Taken by
COMMUNION

Taken by
COMMUNION

How the Lord's Supper Nourishes the Soul

Dan Schmidt

Baker Books

A Division of Baker Book House Co
Grand Rapids, Michigan 49516

© 2003 by Dan Schmidt

Published by Baker Books
a division of Baker Book House Company
P.O. Box 6287, Grand Rapids, MI 49516-6287
www.bakerbooks.com

Printed in the United States of America

Library of Congress Cataloging-in-Publication Data
Schmidt, Dan, 1957–
    Taken by communion : how the Lord's Supper nourishes the soul / Dan Schmidt.
         p.   cm.
    Includes bibliographical references.
    ISBN 0-8010-6455-4 (pbk.)
    1. Lord's Supper. 2. Lord's Supper—Biblical teaching. 3. Bible. N.T. Corinthians, 1st, XI, 23–26—Criticism, interpretation, etc. I. Title.
BV825.3.S36 2004
234′.163—dc22   2003017279

For Jerry and Jane Hawthorne

Shaping hearts and minds,
sharing a gracious table,
showing God.

Contents

Acknowledgments

Several faith communities have shaped my thinking about and practice of communion over the years, and I'm grateful to have been part of such influential local churches in Freeport, Nassau, Wheaton, Princeton, Cincinnati, Laurel, Santiago, Flamingo, and San José.

I'm blessed with a wide web of friends, including those in pastoral ministry like Dave and Belinda, Kevin and Ann, Brian and Grace, Dave and Yvonne, and Carl and Charlene, who encourage me with e-mail, conversation, and cheering of various kinds; they suggest apt books and ask thoughtful questions. Having been refreshed by their generosity, I'm gratified to know they will also be blessed. My life is also consistently enriched by three generations of kids, siblings, cousins, and parents spread across four continents, who offer cheerful support. In this precious family, Sue is most dear.

Grant Osborne and David Dunbar guided early formal study of this topic; more recently John Fawcett, head of public services at the Buswell Memorial Library at Wheaton College, made it possible for me to use the

9

Absheer Room for a few intense days. David Baer, rector of ESEPA Seminary, also made key resources available. People often say, after singing among a large, multiethnic group, that they've had a taste of heaven; I get that sense in libraries. I'm hoping heaven will feature stacks of great books and offer enough time (finally) to read them all.

Introduction

Communion has been part of the church's experience since shortly after Jesus' meal with the disciples in the upper room. The textual, historical, and archaeological record is nearly unbroken from his time to our own, and we know that when the church has gathered in its various forms over the years, these groups have taken communion. No one way of celebrating the Supper has dominated; we find surprising diversity among faith communities. But there is widespread agreement that this ritual is essential for gathered, worshiping followers of Jesus.

We disagree over both practice and theology, and at times the arguments have been bloody. That is a part of church life which those outside the church have difficulty fathoming; it is a wonder that those within the church have grown so comfortable with the infighting. Arguing over the matter of communion has its own irony—the word itself speaks of unity. To be sure, the church has ample room for preferences and even different interpretations of the same biblical texts, but we must become better at valuing one another more than our own precious ideas.

This division isn't new; it was present at that first Last Supper. Judas skulked away to betray the meal's host; other disciples bickered about who deserved highest honor. To some degree we have inherited that underlying discord so that we have a sense of holding the door against a foe eager to break in, of having to eat warily, with vigilance. What makes this posture nearly laughable is that we guard against those who are supposedly friends, neighbors, family. We watch the door for an enemy that is us.

I wonder whether our hearts tilt this way because we approach the table as consumers. Listen to the language common among many at this ritual: We speak of *taking* communion. When we come as takers, we come with the demand of rights high in our throats. This is what we deserve, we say—as we check into a hotel, enter a restaurant, spin through an amusement park's turnstile, or purchase a piece of equipment. If we are takers, it stands to reason that we should receive what we expected and not have to put up with any guff in the process. As takers we anticipate satisfaction and will pounce if it is slow in coming, will jostle to make sure no one takes more than we do. Takers draw lines others must not cross.

Communion is not about taking. Look at the accounts and notice how often Jesus speaks in imperatives. He is in charge, and he draws others in as honored guests. Jesus is the Lord, who *gives*. In his hands, the Supper becomes a parable of grace where God's good gifts flow unchecked. We're meant to recline at this spot and linger in the nourishing presence of the Lord. We come not as *takers of* but as those about to be *taken by* communion.

Much has been written about communion on the technical level. Lengthy treatments have addressed its ties to or differences from Passover and given us analyses of the various biblical accounts; a debate over the meaning of *is* as used by Jesus when referring to bread and wine (e.g., "This is my body" in Matthew 26:26) has spanned centuries and continents. While I am grateful for and informed by a number of these studies, my aim in this book is to engage in a more "devotional" exegesis, probing the biblical texts describing communion and then reflecting on how communion might change people and the churches of which they are part. My sense is that communion has become either too mystical or too familiar and therefore deserves both more understanding and more reverence.

To assist with that, this book will move slowly through one account—that of Paul, found in 1 Corinthians 11. The Synoptic Gospels of Matthew, Mark, and Luke all describe communion, but I am particularly interested here in following Paul because of his conscious effort to address a church. At Corinth they are struggling, making a mess of their newfound faith, and uncertain in their recent transitions. The apostle knows this and meets those struggles head-on. He finds powerful lessons for his present readers in the stories surrounding Passover (see 1 Corinthians 10), especially as he brings attention to bear on the Lord's Supper. Jesus at table is not an occasion for carving another block of theology but for reflecting on common life. Perceiving this event properly has bearing on a community of faith undergoing growing pains.

These Corinthians may have lived long ago and far away, but what they were encountering has a decidedly contemporary ring, for we too are wrestling with how to live out what has captured our hearts and minds. At times we, like those at Corinth, keep to the path before us. At others we list, just as they did. Paul would have them—and us—to be more like those marvelous eye-covered creatures Ezekiel and John described in their revelations so that we would be more likely to see the Lord. We focus, it seems, on other things, like when I visit with people who keep the television on during our conversation: attention keeps slipping from one another to the screen. Or like what is so common as we open our eyes each day after sleeping: we start out with a glimpse of the Lord, and then other things catch us. By bringing communion to prominence for the Corinthians and for us, Paul redirects our gaze to the table and what lies there so that we might see more and see better.

So we will go slowly through this text, landing on terms and phrases.[1] The final two chapters will pick up wording unique to the Gospels but very much in keeping with Paul's understanding; otherwise, we will unpack the Corinthian account. I hope that a reverence for and understanding of the Supper will unfold, encouraging fertile meditation and deep thinking; I hope that lives exposed to the transforming power of grace on display at the table will affect their respective spiritual communities and wider relational webs for the good.

Paul's treatment of communion is set in the wider context of Corinthian worship, an area of "church life" that apparently needed retooling. Again we find common ground with these ancient Christ-followers, for our own approach to worship is in flux; books on and specialists in the topic tell us that change is coming or necessary (or both), and many of us feel that our corporate worship is somewhat adrift. We may not be arguing, like those Corinthians, about idols, sacrifices, head coverings, or particular gifts, but we do know something of discussions—occasionally heated—over music styles, liturgical elements, space, and time. What we don't hear as often is conversation concerning the Supper. Paul's Corinthians had one way of slighting communion; we seem to have found another.

In worship we gather together to draw near to God, who is full of grace—the very grace so vividly displayed by communion. Grace has saved us, and, as we discover so often in worship, it continues to be evident, shaping those who gladly submit to the Lord (see, for example, Rom. 12:6; 1 Cor. 3:10; and the openings of several epistles). Bread and cup take us to a manifestation of grace in the selfless advent and giving of Jesus on behalf of rebels, and they lay in stores of the spiritual enrichment we receive at God's hand. As we eat and drink, our bodies are fueled only modestly in terms of physical nutrition; in spiritual terms, we enter time and space saturated by grace and can be permeated, refreshed, and refueled by it.

We must teach ourselves that coming to this table is as necessary as eating; we must train ourselves to recognize that we require feeding. Too many of us have chosen or fallen into spiritual anorexia or have adopted an unhealthy habit of binging and purging. We have many eating disorders among us when it comes to spiritual food, and so we do well to resume what will promote the health of souls individually and corpo-rately. An important step in this regard is to recognize that our spirits need nourishment and then to satisfy those divinely-prompted cravings with healthy choices. By this our spirits can be prepared for the worship-full life that is pleasing to God, for whose glory we eat and drink (see 1 Cor. 10:31).

You will notice a lot of "we" language as you read this book, because communion links us with God and with each other. To think otherwise is to miss the spirit and point of the celebration. It is not a private affair, nor is it occasion for fracturing the household of faith. I spoke once with a fellow at a worship gathering who did not participate in that evening's communion. He explained: "The denomination in which I was raised does not per-mit us to take communion in other groups." He said this as if I would understand; to this day, I do not. That communion would be a means for division is more than I can grasp in spiritual terms, though it hardly surprises on the human level. There one too easily finds bizarre reasons to disrupt fellowship and justification for doing so. This is wrong. While the "body of the Lord" (1 Cor. 11:29) has a uniformity at its core that permits variety at the edges, we must not assume that this diversity will justify separating ourselves from those whose tastes and preferences differ from our own. We must notice what we share, what we hold in common—and communion, by virtue of the Lord's command, is among such values. Certainly there is room for clumping according to par-ticular inclinations, but we have no grounds for radical separation within the kingdom.

I think three kinds of readers of this book will find themselves drawn in and engaged. First are those whose experience with the church has given them a deep love for, but perhaps a certain fatigue with, practices long-seated in her history. These are those who feel a nagging sense of guilt for thinking something so precious as communion to be rather mundane and who would be open to ways of restoring a flagging interest. If that is the case for you, then my prayer is that reading will trigger renewed vigor for joining the communion.

Second are those called to and tasked with leading worship that includes the celebration of communion. Too often these days "worship" means only music. Can we band together to change the popular definition so that "worship" describes *all* we do during corporate gatherings? Communion is meant to be central when we meet, not a curiosity or one more "worship element" squeezed onto the PowerPoint program. To incorporate communion has implications for everything from traffic flow to Sunday school but deserves our careful consideration.

The third group of readers consists of those who grew up with church intersecting daily life—through forced attendance until high school, or a summer camp experience, or a godly friend or relative—and spent enough time near the center or edges of church life to encounter communion but these days find that it hardly rates attention. You might have started well, but your sincere effort got fouled by small-minded, hard-hearted people, or your days just got too full. And yet there is something that catches you like a hangnail from time to time—like when you do go to a church service, or a wedding, or a first communion. You see that plate and chalice, and it stirs memories long dormant. Or you find yourself, like the French philosopher

Pascal said, wishing it were true. You know yourself to be a spiritual being, you admit to having a spiritual dimension, and you're on the prowl for some assistance. I think this book might open some doors for you.

This is a book about food, a common theme for the Bible. The Garden story includes contention over comestibles; the closing scenes of Revelation speak of a great feast. In between there are banquets and famines, harvests and droughts. The early sacrifice system made much of food offerings. The early church "ate together with glad and sincere hearts" (Acts 2:46).

In Jesus' hands, food took on new meaning. Every meal Jesus participated in that is recorded by a Gospel writer is in some way significant: A miracle or a teaching flows from the table into the heart and mind through the gullet of careful observers. He infuses the mundane with the sublime, and people push away from the tables newly and sometimes strangely filled.

These tables become tableaux for grace, horizontal "screens" depicting dramas played out or messages unfurled for the hungry. Those who come to them find satisfaction, which is how grace operates: It seeks out need and fills it. Tables are good distribution centers for grace, and when Christians after Jesus gathered to "break bread," they were remembering the table where the Lord reclined with his friends.

Bread has been broken among knots of Christians for centuries. The needy and the penitent and the joyful and the hopeful still come, seeking and finding grace. We should be eager for exposure to grace, drink it in, consume all we can. And from the grace so imbibed should come a life characteristic of grace, much as happens when one who eats has strength for pole vaulting, dancing the *merengue,* or prayer.

We forget this too often, perhaps from the sense that we have enough of grace. How could we get more? Why would we want it? This explains, perhaps, our tendency toward junk food in favor of what truly nourishes. It accounts for bouts with fear, selfishness, and doubt. And it stands in contrast to better reports: "Both high and low among men find refuge in the shadow of your wings. They feast on the abundance of your house; you give them drink from your river of delights" (Ps. 36:7–8). David describes the sort of situation I should find myself in more often: reveling in the fullness of God. This vastness, too, is a characteristic of grace. Do I prefer too much the table I set for myself to that of the Lord?

We have company for this preference. Those from whom our spiritual ancestors sprang, who roamed the wilderness after their release from Egypt, often complained of God's meager hospitality and whined about missing other boards. "Can God spread a table in the desert?" they wondered (Ps. 78:19). "Sure, he's done some impressive things, but will the trend continue? Is he good for *today?* Can grace manifest itself *here?*"[2]

Gathering to eat at the Lord's Table reminds us that grace is as common as bread, as sparkling as wine, and as necessary and invigorating as both. We need those reminders, for we live surrounded by an atmosphere rife with noxious poisons and convenience stores stocked only with confections. We need communion, which draws us together to contemplate grace, to be newly infused with grace, to be prepared for demonstrating grace. So to the table we come, and from the table we depart, nourished for life by encounters with the Lord.

The Lord Jesus

Jesus is the Lord. This point is meant, for Christians, to be as obvious as gravity, but typically it gets about as much active attention. That is, we walk, jump, and take care on ladders as though gravity is real and significant, but we rarely pause to consider its influence on our lives. Perhaps this is because gravity's impact is felt only when we fall—then we are aware. Is it the same with "the Lord"? Do we cry out and find him then, count on him then, curse him then? Is he a daily, active concern?

The *Lord*. This word has an ancient ring, dredged from the feudal systems we studied in high school or the ruined castles we visited on vacation. We hear it the way equatorial people receive "snow," wondering how it fits with present experience. Paul helps. He uses the word hundreds of times, more frequently even than "Jesus." It is a title more than a name; it is a description, an invitation, a challenge, a charge, a hope. By referring to Jesus in these terms, Paul forces the issue of loyalty; his repetition soaks us like a tropical rainstorm. For people who are simultaneously fiercely proud and frighteningly dependent, "Lord" illumines a path toward sanity and peace. This is because it holds out the prospect of guidance and leadership. We are suspicious of both, of course, because of our training and experience. But we are eager for each, too, and in our hearts yearn for the trustworthy guide and the benevolent leader.

The Lord is both, which surprises us more than it should. We're like children, who regularly seem baffled when they hit the ground after a slip on the rug or the ice. *That hurt,* their faces say, their brains unwilling to accept that gravity's downward pull, combined with the electromagnetic force holding the ground beneath them together, yields the same result every time. Our childlike response to the Lord is similar: Guide? Leader? Really?

The children of God down through the ages have had difficulty recognizing, serving, obeying, loving, and enjoying the Lord. To live under his leadership in his kingdom has provoked us. That was the case during the captivity of Israel's offspring in Egypt and remains the case centuries later. Jesus knew of this struggle with lordship and so gave his followers a variety of means for reflecting on it and being confronted by it. One of those came during a poignant farewell evening with his closest friends, during a meal we now call the communion, the Eucharist, or the Lord's Supper. It was around this table that he meant for people—then and now—to notice and be captivated by the Lord.

Alan's path crossed mine in college, and we became friends later as his missionary zeal blossomed. His passion was for relief work and for training local people in appropriate technology. In the Dominican Republic he built an enormous, intricate aquarium that supported fish, fowl, and plant life. Part of his house shared a wall with the aquarium, so he put in a window at floor level. That way kids inside his house could watch what was going on inside the tank. Nearby he started a smelting operation, scavenging abandoned engines for aluminum to make kitchen utensils. In another place he cultivated an unusual local chile pepper for export and showed builders how to fashion windows out of discarded glass bottles. Alan made friends with specialists; he sucked knowledge out of books and magazines. "Find fanatics," he counseled, a gleam in his eye over some new project. "You can always learn from a fanatic."

We think of fanatics in negative terms: they are the mad scientists, the sports nuts, the computer geeks, the garage guitarists. Alan stressed a different dimension by emphasizing the fanatic's single-minded devotion to a task or topic. Under this definition Paul was a fanatic, captivated by his Lord, Jesus. "I preach Christ," he insisted, as though anyone who knew him would have been unclear about Paul's preferred subject matter. "I want to know Christ." "I am his prisoner, his apostle, richly blessed by him." "For me, to live is Christ." Statements like these make clear Paul's interest and motivation. He was dedicated, focused, consumed.

Paul's fanatical interest in Jesus jumps off the pages of his letters. One simply cannot read more than a few sentences before hearing about Jesus. At times a line of reasoning is interrupted because an earlier thought, having directed Paul to his Lord, is abandoned in favor of praise for or wonder at Jesus. That challenges students learning Greek: How does Paul move from *here* to *here* grammatically? they wonder. It can confuse those engaged in "inductive" Bible study too. But read more emotionally than rationally, and Paul's path makes sense: Jesus is never far from his view, and he needs little prompting to launch another paean.

The Gospel writers reserve "Lord" for a handful of occasions, usually to stress the sudden "aha!" of a new convert or young disciple. It gets a more complete workout in subsequent documents, especially by Paul. For him, the proper name (Jesus) tends to fade in favor of the titles "Christ" or "Lord." This gives both familiarity and reverence, as Paul speaks of One he knows well who is also supreme. We glimpse this in our own experience when a companion introduces us to Governor/Judge/ Professor/Doctor So-and-So, a person of accomplishment or notoriety. Paul does not brag but pulls others in with his own awe and delight. "Let me tell you about Jesus," he would say, knocked out by the Lord, eager for others to know him better.

The Corinthians were in danger of losing the Lord. Perhaps the pervasive pantheism of their day encouraged them to view Jesus like other available deities, or maybe it was an active hostility against followers of "the Way" or simply the press of ordinary routine and responsibility. Whatever the cause, the effect was noticeable, and they were behaving like those for whom the Lord was as relevant as cheese. They needed a fanatic like Paul, one who roundly criticizes their actions and then calls them to look at Jesus again. "Remember what I told you about him?" he asks. "It was based on what he told me. Let's review that together." And then the apostle proceeds to recount the tale—and the significance—of that final meal. He mentions the Lord often in this short paragraph (1 Cor. 11:23–26). "Get this," he urges his friends in Corinth. "Live worthy of, aware of, the Lord."

I think of people whose jobs demand a punishing routine: A blizzard of e-mail awaits them each morning; decisions involving huge sums and many employees must be swift and accurate; nights on airplanes and in hotels are common. I think of people whose families press them: Medical or psychological concerns weigh heavily; past memories haunt; terrible choices in the present upset delicate balances. Then I consider the teenagers: Hormones, genetic legacies, and peer groups wrestle them; they live days, weeks, or months isolated from constructive influences; they are bombarded by suspect data. Lives like these get dominated by so many concerns, and the Lord (an English word from the Latin *dominus*) takes a back seat.

Our congregation was given a church building by another group when dwindling numbers made their keeping the place untenable. We moved in one weekend and began exploring and cleaning. In one corner we found a storage closet full of dusty furniture and files. Tucked behind a cabinet was an artist's rendering of Jesus, one of those standard church hallway portraits with the beard, wavy hair, and sad eyes. Its hiddenness caught me. The picture was cobwebbed, even dirty, and far from view. I don't tend to favor this sort of depiction, but it struck me how easy it was to bury the Lord.

The Lord. Who will be Lord in my life, in yours? How will the Lord make himself known? How will we show him? Will we be fickle in our affections toward the Lord? The monk Benedict encouraged disciples of the Lord to break the daily routine at several points in order to refocus their attention on the Lord with prayer and *lectio divina;*[1] I try to build this into my life and inevitably forget. The phone rang, a child appeared with a question, a sermon beckoned, a beautiful or stormy day demanded notice, a fingernail needed filing, a grudge needed nurturing—and the Lord? Tomorrow. Maybe.

This struggle over lordship started long ago. As Adam and Eve strolled through the Garden, they saw a tree that symbolized the Lord. "Avoid this one," he had instructed. "Eat other fruit instead." The wheedling serpent keyed in on this prohibition. "What's so bad here?" that creature asked. "You're right," those people replied, "it isn't bad at all." They took, ate, and suddenly became aware of a shift in the universe. A previously unquestioned Lord now stood on a pedestal deeply fissured by doubt.

That tree's fruit raised a question about lordship. Millennia after Adam and Eve left the Garden, Jesus would sit with disciples around that upper room's table. Pointing to bread and wine, he asks, "Who is your Lord?"

Who is Jesus? Pass by the pious portraiture hung on cinder blocks or printed in Sunday school papers. Let the alliterated sermons languish for a moment. Suspend the bookstore jargon and the coffee mug slogans, which tend to be as detailed and accurate as middle schoolers sharing information on sex. Instead, let God's Spirit guide you.

The Spirit speaks to those with "ears to hear" in tones both subtle and bold. That urgency you feel to find the truth that is "out there," that insistence on justice that rises in the face of gross inhumanity, that sense of a preacher speaking directly to you, that longing for a true friend or stable home, that bubble of joy at a constructive exchange, that gasp of awe at a sunrise or starfish, that rush of hope, that certainty of insight, that need for peace, that demand for love—this is the Spirit. We can cobble together substitutes for the Spirit, wanting a quicker or easier or more predictable satisfaction for these deep desires. We might shove the Spirit away once we recognize that truth and beauty tend to hurt before they heal. It is possible, too, that we might welcome God's Spirit. That might require pushing back the furniture decorating our cluttered lives; it might involve learning to like new music. As we try a few steps "in the Spirit," perhaps we will wobble, perhaps we will feel slightly off-balance, but then soon we are likely to discover ourselves walking and leaping and praising God.

This was Paul's hope as he spoke to people whose hearts had been captured by the grace of Jesus. The apostle's fervent prayer was that many would "keep in step with the Spirit" (Gal. 5:25) and move decisively, intentionally, extensively. "You began in the Spirit," Paul would say, "with your faith sealed. Stay there, where the Spirit can keep marking you." When you hear other voices, when you find yourself gathering interests like lint, when you hit an atmosphere composed of elements opposed to God and find it difficult to breathe, seek the Spirit. Make a point of listening, too, for God's Spirit is active, engaged, aware.

I recommended a woman for a board position with an agency on the brink of making a wider impact. After the election she shook my hand: "Thanks for giving me the opportunity to serve." That's Spirit-talk, an awareness of a voice calling one to things other than self-interest. Another responded favorably to an invitation to preach:

"I'd be honored," she said. She is not proud, seeking occasion to vaunt her skill; she is Spirit-led, attentive.

Scripture helps us meet Jesus as well. Start with the Gospels and discover how both light scanning and deep study[2] reward curiosity, enhance understanding, and provoke constructive questions: Why is so much repeated? What is going on with these parables, and miracles, and prayers? What is Jesus telling us as he teaches his disciples? Where is the Gospels' attention focused? The Gospels are not simple biographies, tracing the birth, life, and death of a notable figure. They draw us into the world of One totally unlike any other and show what happens when he intersects with humanity. From these books we learn what God is like, and we come to terms with the limitations of our understanding. We read about others who confront the Lord and those he confronts, and from these encounters we uncover much of our own hearts, learning what it is like to wrestle with or gladly come under the Lord. The Gospels explain the background for the later events of Acts and serve as the mother lode for letter writers like Paul, John, James, and Peter. No one of them can exhaustively handle the experiences and activities of Jesus; as John says, "If every one of them were written down, I suppose that even the whole world would not have room for the books that would be written" (John 21:25). Still, faced with a daunting task, they write away, laboring to convey his character, behavior, and motivations. They succeed, and we are blessed.

A third source of information about the Lord is people already under his care. I've had the privilege of watching a Bible college professor change focus to pastor a needy church, of breakfasting with a couple who re-entered active ministry because they thought retirement in their late seventies was too early, of receiving e-mail from one who was deemed too old for the classroom but became immersed in research to write commentaries for a new generation of scholars. I've met with pastors and missionaries at the midpoint of their careers; our times together are almost breathless because of the press of responsibility. I've watched teachers work through texts at a glacial pace. I hear from corporate executives, chemists, secretaries, mechanics, programmers, and real estate brokers who are committed to living out kingdom values. I talk with high schoolers, college students, and those on the front edge of independent life about what's happening now and what might soon break open. We scheme, plan, dream, pray. I find or have recommended books that are filled with insights garnered from deep reflection or experience in the trenches. I am often bowled over by the many who have gladly put their lives under the Lord. They model, teach, point, encourage.

When the call comes to "follow" this Lord, it is an invitation to unwrap the personal security blankets that often muffle his voice or blur our vision. Like the man once lame, we rise and walk along the path the Lord is traveling. The overarching challenge of this invitation is to release our innate commitment to personal sovereignty and gratefully, sincerely welcome a new Lord. As we do that, we enter the life of worship where we gladly lift the Lord to his rightful place and gladly render him his due. We listen eagerly for and to his voice; we open the heart and bow the knee.

J. R. R. Tolkien's *Lord of the Rings* trilogy tells the story of two brothers, Boromir and Faramir. Boromir, the oldest, joins the fledgling company of four hobbits, an elf, a dwarf, a man, and a wizard intending to destroy "the One Ring"; he is a representative of men and the next Steward of Gondor, a fortress held against the opposing evil lord. Boromir appears to be a formidable ally, but his heart is divided between serving the fellowship of the ring and pursuing his own goals. Eventually Boromir's duplicity is his undoing, and he dies shortly after trying to steal the ring for himself.

Tolkien gives us in Faramir one whose heart is true. When first introduced, Faramir is stern, almost harsh, to the hobbits who stumble on his secret lair. Then we discover that it is not anger or pride driving him, like his elder brother, but a single-minded, almost fanatical devotion.[3] As Tolkien's trilogy draws to its dramatic conclusion, Faramir rides at the head of one army, having expressed his unqualified allegiance to the true lord, Aragorn. The latter's triumph is Faramir's as well, possible in large measure because of fanatical devotion like Faramir's.

In the battles we face, be they vitriolic encounters with unsheathed persecution or the more subtle snares of daily indifference toward what we hold dear, the pressure to capitulate on our allegiance to the Lord is extraordinary. Little wonder so many fade in their enthusiasm for him. But then we discover those whose loyalty, once formed, is fierce. Visit Joshua's camp, for instance, as that emerging leader listened first to Moses, and then to the people, and then to God, all telling him to buck up and get on with his responsibilities. The chorus of voices is enough to persuade him, and we read of Joshua's incredible, repeated triumphs against impossible odds. "Be strong and courageous," the Lord enjoins, ". . . for the LORD your God will be with you wherever you go" (Josh. 1:9). Still, Joshua must decide: Will he believe what God is saying? As the story progresses we see quite clearly that for Joshua, God is Lord. At the end of his life, Joshua stands before the people he has led, urging them to bow before the Lord as well. "Choose today whom you will serve," he bellows. "Will it be the foreign gods such as we have met in battle? As for me and mine, we will serve the Lord" (see Josh. 24:15).

Serving the Lord is what brings trouble. The people standing beneath Joshua's strident challenge could glibly promise their fealty. "We will serve the LORD our God and obey him," they might claim (Josh. 24:24). But under pressure imposed by foreign threats and the incessant nibbling of nearby attractions, their zeal withered. Their promises about serving the Lord had the durability of strawberries; within a couple of generations, Jacob's children had abandoned the Lord.

We are painfully similar. When the church I serve gathers, we pray regularly for the "persecuted church" scattered around the globe and often forced underground. We remember those for whom the expression of faith spells difficulty for relationships, careers, families, and health. More recently we are adding to these intercessions on behalf of believers living where politics are calm, economics stable, diversions plentiful, and options for spirituality common. There the church struggles not with developing strategies for survival but with remembering that it is still relevant. "What need have we of *you?*" the fat and happy society asks this church in different ways. In such environments muttered half-hearted answers are dreadfully easy. It becomes common to believe the notices posted about the church's increasing irrelevance, to start looking at the Lord and saying "Whatever."

How does one buck this trend? How does one come back off the beach, set down the cooler, and brush away the sand of a comfortable, unthreatened existence? How does one welcome the Lord, stay with the Lord, follow the Lord? It starts with devotion and obedience.

Neither is genetic, like curly hair or hammer toes. In fact, welcoming a Lord who is not us into our lives entails the sort of submission we are genetically disposed to resist. It takes practice, dedication. To devote ourselves to this God and then to obey him is about the most unnatural thing we can do. This is why we must take our cues not from TV, CDs, and stock reports but from the Spirit, the Word, and tested guides. As we pause to listen, we will begin to hear, however faintly, the music that draws us in. Confidence will grow, and success will come. Then will follow testing, and discipline. Will we give him our hearts? Will we still obey? Those questions will be asked daily, hourly, and each time, at each fork, we will have to frame a reply.

And when we say yes to the Lord, what then? Look to the disciples around that table on that night. "I'm yours," each said, promising faith. Then Judas gets up to leave. Later, in the Garden, the rest flee. Obedience, dependability, a fixedness—even for people who spent hours with Jesus, these were hard to come by. When pushed, they crumbled. But only one disintegrated. For the others, failure was temporary, and we find that by the time of Acts these followers have a renewed sense of determination that steels them for the life ahead. They are fixed then, weighted by their attachment to the Lord.

For Christmas one year I received one of those inflatable "punching clowns" with sand at the base. You strike the clown and it goes down, only to spring back up for another blow. As kids, we thought this a hoot: A blow to the head only meant another opportunity to hit it again. After a few more years passed, this clown started to resemble what so many I knew were facing in getting slapped by a culture, a friend, a church member. When the thumping comes, it seems only prudent to stay down or roll away. But one reads, notices, talks, listens—and uncovers more of what lordship encompasses. So those who take into full account the demands and expectations of submission to Jesus come up again, knowing a little better what to expect but not ready to quit the scene. In this they remind me of another childhood game: tetherball, where opponents strike a volleyball that is strung to a tall pole. Each successful blow in this game brings the ball that much closer to the pole and the player to victory.

It is devotion that gives us weight and makes us able to recover from every impact. It is obedience that tethers us to the Lord himself, such that when we are struck, we only move closer to him. It is the simple, determined yes to the Lord that forms devotion, displays obedience, and results in a life of glad submission, which in turn earns his approval. The night ahead of these disciples will be long and grim and will reveal hearts unable to withstand pressure. But the days that follow will bring about a renewed devotion that puts everything at the feet of Jesus. These disciples and their spiritual heirs will gladly face with equal strength both danger and apathy. They will learn to practice obedience daily, and they will prove to themselves and to others who is their Lord.

Two

On the Night

The chronology of Jesus' final week is a matter of dispute. A few time-markers help us, but puzzles remain. Among these is the question of when the Supper occurred. Was it on Passover, as the Synoptic Gospels say, or was it *not* Passover, as John's record intimates? Scholars have wrestled with an answer, and along the way some ingenious solutions have been proposed. But few disagree with the conclusion that Jesus' last meal with his disciples happened in Jerusalem at least very near the celebration of Passover, and that influence on their dinner is informative. For when Jesus sits at the table with his friends, they are together breathing air charged with memories of Egypt. Long ago their ancestors had been released because of a miraculous salvation; God's grace had run like a river carrying them to safety. On this night, in this city of peace, the grace of God would again be in focus, because another miraculous rescue was about to unfurl.

God's people had entered Egypt at Joseph's invitation following an area-wide famine. Incredibly, they stayed another four centuries. For a while the people found their surroundings tolerable, even pleasant, especially in comparison with the barren country they had left. Previously nomadic people stayed put, but gradually their surroundings decayed. Like limestone before a sandstorm, the contributions of Joseph eroded as new Pharaohs, intent on maintaining the dynasty, pursued nationalistic concerns. Those Joseph had brought to Goshen were increasingly marginalized until four centuries later another leader, "who did not know about Joseph" (Exod. 1:8), came to power, and they were perceived as a threat.

Benign indifference became intentional persecution, and Jacob's children were now the enemy. Rather than being valued for the contribution they might have made to the commonweal, the children of Israel were viewed with suspicion and alarm. So this new Pharaoh took: He robbed their future by taking their baby boys, and he ruined their efficiency by taking the very building materials that were used for Egypt's benefit. In the reign of this Pharaoh, life ground down to the nub; the people had no hope.

Finally they began to cry out for relief, and their howls reached God. He sent Moses with news of his interest in their plight. It was a welcome message, and the people "bowed down and worshiped" (Exod. 4:31) when they heard of God's concern for their welfare. But the impact of this good news faded quickly under the bright lights of "discouragement and cruel bondage" aimed by Pharaoh (Exod. 6:9). Speaking to that leader on God's behalf, Moses tried to stop the harsh treatment and met only resistance. So the plagues began. After aggravating the Egyptians mercilessly, the Lord finally drove down hard, slaying each family's firstborn. Only those who carefully followed his instructions escaped the terrible judgment of the climactic tenth plague.

When faithful householders painted their doorways with blood from a young lamb, the killing angel God sent to slay all firstborn would "pass over" those homes, preserving all inside. The arrogant who ignored this requirement suffered; the obedient found their families and livestock intact later that dark night. It was these people who, after following God's directive, now scurried after Moses out of Egypt, where their people had been enslaved for 430 years. Slowing that night only to pack their meager belongings and divest neighbors of trinkets and apparel needed for nomadic life, they ate a quick meal of roasted lamb and flat bread.

To ensure that night would not be lost in other events, God used this Passover to recalibrate the Jewish year. Subsequent calendars would celebrate Passover as the first of the annual feasts, two weeks into the new year. It was meant to be repeated, a "lasting ordinance" (Exod. 12:17) remembered by ensuing generations.

Enthusiasm waned. Scripture records several Passovers during the desert sojourn and conquest of Canaan, and then it is eerily quiet on the subject. Mention returns in 2 Chronicles 30, when Hezekiah purifies the Temple and reinstates Passover as part of the routine. Remarkably, the practice dies with him and is not revived until Hezekiah's great-grandson Josiah ascends the throne and later guides his nation back to the ancient ritual. The commentary is notable: "The Passover had not been observed like this in Israel since the days of the prophet Samuel; and none of the kings of Israel had ever celebrated such a Passover as did Josiah, with the priests, the Levites and all Judah and Israel who were there" (2 Chron. 35:18). The chronological record shudders to a stop in the next chapter as, a few years later, accumulated disobedience brought on the nation's exile and the ruin of Jerusalem. The Temple went down too, and with its destruction, Passover lambs had nowhere to be slaughtered.

So there is another long silence, broken when the exiles return to Israel and under Haggai and Zechariah rebuild the Temple (see Ezra 6:19–22). This is the last Passover celebration we know of from Scripture until the Gospel accounts in the New Testament. There we discover that Passover has become firmly entrenched in the life of Israel. It has also undergone some significant changes. Mass gatherings to celebrate Passover corporately have been replaced by family units meeting in homes to prepare and eat the meal while reclining at a table. A particular way of understanding and sharing the story has developed.[1] Wine is commonly served.

The tale of Passover is as ancient as a myth, based on an event thirty-four centuries old. It is as widely known, too; aspects of this epic journey find mention in more than half of the Bible's sixty-six books. It's one of those memories that lingers, like having a root canal or getting married. "Egypt" was like that, an evocative time and place capable of kindling positive and negative recollections. What Walter Brueggemann calls the "normative narrative" received an annual retelling as each subsequent generation was reminded of what happened in Egypt, the desert, and the Promised Land.

That first hasty meal is replaced with a lengthy feast; the furtiveness of a people on the move folds into a relaxed gathering around the table, where diners have the leisure to recline. That there is a table at all suggests domestication, and the presence of wine indicates that former slaves are now amply provisioned and free. Hope flavors the meal like a spice, encouraging celebrants to anticipate release from foreign occupation and life in God's company.

Passover encompassed both the dominated and the disenfranchised with the message of God's provision. He knew, he cared, and he offered what was needed. So Passover participants sit and stare, faced with evidence of God's generosity. Foods in quantities usually rare now make the table groan. Wine, a drink for the wealthy, flows freely. Variety and opulence remind diners that God is good, that Jehovah Jireh moves when his people are in need. For those with eyes on deeper matters, provision of temporal needs points to the God who is even more concerned with spiritual needs. The One who can bring food, money, and clothing can also attend to the soul—as he did, long ago, when he entered a hopeless situation and engineered a release.

Passover tracks this rescue. The Jews had been oppressed and enslaved, living in the shadow of a despot who used and discarded them like cheap tools. In this Pharaoh resembled Satan on the prowl, ready to hurt, control, and ultimately destroy (see 1 Peter 5:8). At first, the people are too blind to comprehend their plight. Then Moses comes, a hero sent by God. He guides them safely across the sea, out of harm's way, where they finally realize that the Lord saved them (Exod. 14:30). Then they break out in triumphant song, ebullient at their release (Exod. 15:1–21). Just before he dies, Moses recalls that night with a mixture of awe and wonder: "Who is like you, a people saved by the LORD?" (Deut. 33:29). They are known as the rescued, their identity tied to the Lord who saved them.

Rescue stories cross cultures and span generations. Hearts race and pulses pound when we hear or read such tales. Take Derek Lundy's account of the 1996–97 Vendée Globe, a circumnavigation of the planet below 40 degrees latitude by solo sailors. The race began in France with sixteen contestants; the winner took nearly 106 days to complete the course. Along the way, one sailor and his boat were lost, and several others experienced severe difficulties. Three capsized in southern seas and were left helpless. Others went looking for them.

Raphaël Dinelli skippered one of the boats that flipped. He scrambled to the slippery deck and waited. Eventually a search plane dropped a raft, but Dinelli was alone, his nearest help the skipper of another sailboat 160 miles downwind. When radioed of the desperate situation, Pete Goss decided to turn around, at great personal cost, to face the fierce gale and attempt to find Dinelli. It was no simple feat. For three days Goss would beat his way through drenching waves the height of 6-story buildings and repeatedly struggle up peaks to the crest where, according to Derek Lundy's account,

> the full force of the wind accelerates the boat down the 50-foot slope of the wave into the next trough.
>
> Goss couldn't open his eyes to windward and it was difficult to breathe. The noise was unrelenting and deafening, at a decibel level approaching that of a nearby

jet engine. In gusts, the wind blew well into the range of hurricane force. . . .

As his boat made its slow, concussive progress, climbing one mountain after another, Goss kept wondering if it would hold together.

An Australian air force plane helped Goss locate Dinelli's life raft, and Goss finally managed to wrestle the French sailor into his own boat.

He was stiff as a board and could barely move by himself. Then Goss realized how far gone Dinelli was. He rolled him over on his back. "All you could see was his eyes," Goss said. "And it was just . . . the emotion in the pair of eyes was just amazing, really. He was trying to say 'Thank you, thank you'; he couldn't really talk. He was very cold."[2]

Two other sailors would be pulled from disaster; their experiences were equally harrowing. One reads, absolutely gripped, for rescues thrill us. We love the stories of heroes who face overwhelming odds and emerge victorious—plucking a sailor from the sea, carrying a child out of the burning building, or leading a group of newly emancipated prisoners. Rescues quicken our hearts and minds because deep down we know that we too are lost and trapped people; in our quiet moments we know how desperate our own situation is. We long for heroes, from the Greek Titans to *The Matrix's* Neo, who will take note of our condition and step into our helplessness with strength and grace to do what is necessary to engineer our release.

Sometimes the cost of rescue gets overlooked. We are so gripped by the need, or so elated by the outcome, that we forget the sacrifice a rescue so often requires. This explains why Jesus selects only two dishes from the laden Passover table to talk about. He wants his disciples to remember the sacrifice that was part of this wonderful story.

Jesus assumed the role customarily given to the family's head in telling and interpreting Passover for those around the table.[3] When he deviated from the well-known script by using different words with the bread and cup, the disciples would have noticed—but then they were familiar with Jesus' tendency to change the way a passage was typically handled. "You have heard it said . . . ," he would begin on various occasions and then offer an alternative reading on a law that had become mired in tradition (see, for example, Matt. 5:21, 27, 33, 38, 43). In those instances, Jesus was drawing people deeper, trying to help them look more closely than simple repetition of accepted applications encouraged. "What did God mean by this?" he was asking. "What is the heart of the matter?"

The same was happening on this special night. Venerable tradition deferred to Jesus' own interpretation, allowing him to explain what from the earliest times had been known as "the LORD's Passover" (see, for example, Exod. 12:11, 48; Lev. 23:5; Num. 9:10, 14). With the Lord before them now, the disciples hear a fresh rendering of the story. In recalling Egypt, attention ran easily to the dispatched enemy and all the perks freedom afforded; Jesus wants to make sure that his disciples understand that this victory began with sacrifice.

It was not enough to look through Passover to the powerful overthrow of a hated enemy, nor to chortle over one's newfound release. Passover's rescue required sacrifice: you did not leave Egypt intact unless a lamb was slaughtered and drained. Holding bread and cup, Jesus pulls the emphasis on sacrifice back to center stage. He is about to be torn open and poured out, he tells these disciples, so that another rescue can occur.

Jesus had already upset the evening's equilibrium by washing the disciples' feet. This was the work of servants, not the lord, but Jesus had to capture attention long lost to custom and repetition. "Do you see what I've done for you?" he asks. He is not above stooping; Jesus comes to serve. He will gladly take up the basin and towel, just as he will gladly go to the cross to save people from a terrible enemy.

That this lesson sank in for the early church is reflected in an early hymn that circulated widely. In this hymn, which Paul included in his letter to the Philippians (Phil. 2:6–11),[4] we see how Jesus' followers made the connection between service and power. As the stanzas proclaim, the servant's heart shatters sin's manacles. By choosing to pour himself out, Jesus positions himself to save. At an earlier time God took Israel by the hand and carved a path for the nation to follow. In the latter days Jesus, who stooped to wash feet, blazed with humility a quite different sort of trail. The story in his hands comes out differently, but better. This is a night to ponder rescues fully.

Passover actually speaks of two rescues. The first happened more than three millennia ago, when meek Moses marched at the front of a long line of Jacob's offspring from Egypt to the border of Canaan. This is the story told each year in a multi-sensory evening when the currents of history blend with the texture of food sprawling across a table.

There is a second, more subtle rescue as well.

When we remember, when we go back to Exodus for that tale of people beaten down by Pharaoh and rescued by God, what else comes to mind? The terrible retribution that fell on the unfaithful. What else? The way the ancestors despoiled the Egyptians, taking their food, clothes, and money. What else? The opening of the sea and the destruction of that enormous army!

What else?

You must remember this: In the desert, the people moaned and whined and complained. They repeatedly turned away from the God who came for them. They made a mockery of what was sacred to him. Do you recall the golden calf?

Sitting at the Passover table each year is supposed to vividly raise the memory that God did not break faith even when his people did. Remember: While this was a time when God's awesome power was on display, when the world's greatest ruler was reduced to fish food, the people toward whom God showed great favor could hardly contain their contempt. "We miss the leeks and onions of Egypt," they complained. "We'd rather go back."

The annual celebration of Passover includes the recitation of God's great good on behalf of his people. It also gives the lesson of this people's great disgrace as they blamed God for the ardor of the journey. If you are called to celebrate the former every year, you will not miss the latter. And when that happens, you are likely to grow hard, or heavy, bent down by guilt.

So remember: Passover is a rescue story.

The great wonder of grace is that it doesn't keep track of stupidity and act only when the count is low. The glorious message of Passover is that God comes to people who are more needy than deserving; they haven't earned the right to God's miracles by the sheer weight of their goodness. Rather, these people are desperate in every sense. If God doesn't come, they will sink, literally and figuratively, in the muddy brick pits. But he does, and they don't. He lifts them up and leads them out, the whole bitter lot of them. Their whines fill the desert air; more than once, God threatens to undo them. Moses prevails, and grace wins out, and the people survive. But the memory of their foolish complaints is a memory each annual celebration of Passover preserves.

Such memory might undo a person, its weight crushing a heart with guilt. Except that this is a rescue. Remember? Passover might easily stop at the edges of Egypt, once Israel steps over the threshold into the wilderness. Instead it spans what led up to the rescue and what followed. It reminds us all that even when God steps in, we can still be idiots.

Satan can use such a realization to hector us with guilt. We might succumb to this, or we can resist him, standing firm in the realization that the One who came to our rescue by snapping our captor's chains also relieves us of the load of guilt we might be inclined to carry. True, even after the grace of rescue we still act ungratefully. But true as well, God does not leave us; he stays as guide into the promised land. And so from this too we are released: the burden of guilt created by our willful rebellion.

Passover shows the power of God to bend nature to his will, to shatter a ruler like Pharaoh and the army under his command, to wrest a million people from their familiar routine and provide for them during decades of hostile circumstances. Passover tells the story of God's power to rescue, and so forms exactly the right backdrop for Jesus' passion. We know that his whole life was focused on his necessary death, and so it stands to reason that the time of that death, like every other detail, was intentional. Why? Because that death was essential for the plan to unfold. He had come, remember, to rescue, like God had done before in Egypt.

This time the stakes are higher. There are many more people, culled from every nation, race, tongue, and tribe, stuck like stamps under the thumb of a ruthless oppressor. And success means not a temporary deed to desirable real estate but eternity with almighty God.

This time the sacrifice is greater as well: the lamb is God's own Son, who willingly lays down his life. "Do you understand what I've done?" Jesus asks. Once he had washed their feet, this question set a tone for what would follow, for this evening would stretch the disciples far past what they had grasped up to this point. They had come expecting a drawn-out evening to eat good food, sing old songs, and rehearse the familiar story of Moses and the Exodus. But Jesus was pushing them into deeper water.

Jesus takes up the bread and cup nestled among so much else on the table they surrounded. "This," he says, "is for you. Remember your ancestors as you enter this story afresh. Recall their rescue as they left Egypt under God's mighty hand. But think too of this: the release you needed and need still from your own sin and guilt. It happens, as is always the case in a rescue, because of sacrifice." This sacrifice was hinted at when the evening's festivities began and would be fully made in a matter of hours.

Who is a people like you? Moses asked this of those who reaped the benefit of the first Passover; now Jesus could raise the same question among those following him to freedom. He could answer the same way, too: "You are a people saved by the Lord. So come," he would say as the evening's host, "and enjoy the freedom you now have because God has sent a hero on your behalf. And go, knowing that once this night has passed, you will be telling the rescue story to those still in captivity."

Three

He Was Betrayed

Tables, like fire, have potential for both good and ill. Diners get food poisoning even at fancy restaurants: they go in good faith expecting a good meal and receive instead great pain. We ate fish one night in our own home and had to call a doctor when one child began choking on a translucent bone. A decade has passed, but even fresh trout still makes her pause. Danger—as any parent knows—lurks on a table. And then, besides the physical threats from the food and implements, there are the diners themselves: What rattles about in them? Is there any whiff of irritation or disloyalty among the participants of the meal, as when Judas's betrayal scented the air at Jesus' final Passover?

Jesus sits to dine among friends, vulnerable. He has come with eager anticipation (Luke 22:15); he must also have known what the rest of the evening would hold. So he would join the fellowship around that festive meal, but he would also be looking into the eyes of one who would turn the tables and give him up. There is nourishment to be had at this board, but disaster is on the menu, too.

"You prepare a table before me in the presence of my enemies," said one of Jesus' ancestors (Ps. 23:5). Did Jesus recall David's experience as he entered that upper room? King David was surrounded by peril much of his adult life: wild beasts, government officials, neighboring rulers, family members—there were many conspirators nearby as he walked a narrow path, surely aware of and bent by dangers both obvious and concealed. Jesus tasted the same. His public life was much briefer than David's, but of similar intensity. Like David, Jesus evoked passionate responses; like David, he stirred the base instincts of many hearts. When Jesus comes to Jerusalem for Passover, enemies are lurking like panthers, biding their time but sure to strike. One predator slips into the room and eases onto a rug to recline at table with the Lord.

Each Gospel lists the disciples Jesus called to join him in traveling through Israel for three years. These lists vary a bit, using some different names for the same people or shifting the order in which particular men are mentioned. But there are some fixed points in each: Peter always comes first. Judas always comes last.[1] The scant data on Judas has provoked various speculations in print and on film; less colorful and more severe, the biblical text tells us three things about him.

First, he was a traitor. Nearly every mention of Judas, from his introduction as one of Jesus' Twelve (Matt. 10:4) to the closing scene of his death (Matt. 27:3), includes some reference to his betrayal of Jesus. The Gospels are careful to show that Judas's treachery was not accidental. He contracts with religious authorities to "hand him over" and is methodical in selecting the best occasion for that (Matt. 26:15–16). As an "insider" Judas would know where and when Jesus would be both accessible and away from crowds that might otherwise resist his arrest (see John 18:2–5; Acts 1:16).

Second, he was a thief. Contemporary entertainment has done much to make thieves admirable rogues; in biblical terms, stealing is deplorable. Judas, keeper of the communal moneybag (John 12:4–6), dipped repeatedly into the group's funds for private use. His freedom to do so indicated a seared conscience or a callous indifference. That he covered his greed with the deceit of care for the poor on at least one occasion made his acts all the more heinous.

Third, he was an apostate. Given opportunity to turn, like any other, from self to God, Judas chose instead to join Jesus' company without sharing in his Spirit.[2] Judas gave more room to Satan than to Jesus, so that the enemy's prompts were heeded (John 13:2) and his entrance permitted (Luke 22:3). After he died, the apostolic witness was that Judas went "where he belongs" (Acts 1:25), as was fitting for the "one doomed to destruction" (John 17:12). That said, we should be able to close the book on this simple though tragic tale.

But press that point: Has Jesus in his high-priestly prayer (John 17) condemned Judas out of hand? Is it the case that the deck was stacked, the lines were drawn, and he never had a chance? Perhaps. It is possible that God simply pre-selected a traitor who would hand Jesus over to the authorities. It is also possible that Judas is like others whose lives are tracked in Scripture so that we can follow both decision and consequence.

51

Take Cain, called like his brother Abel to sacrifice before God. Cain responds on his own terms and brings what is not pleasing to the Lord. Abel's efforts, however, are acceptable, and this aggravates Cain. God speaks to him, warning about the sin "crouching at your door" (Gen. 4:7). Sin's desire for capturing Cain is strong, though not inevitable; Cain can master it. But instead of recognizing his shortcomings and admitting his failure, he becomes sullen and resistant, opening a door for sin's entrance. Cain succumbs and kills Abel; still, the Lord does not abandon him. Cain stays under God's merciful protection even when he "went out from the presence of the LORD" (Gen. 4:16). His story ends with two notes: the wanderer settles, becoming a city-builder, and the obstinate ruffian calls his firstborn Enoch, a name derived from a Hebrew noun that signifies submission and dedication. Both indicate a profound change of heart.[3]

Others are warned by God of imminent destruction, like the Pharaoh met by Moses. As happened with Cain, this leader was told in advance about the danger of disobedience and given opportunity to recant. He softened temporarily (see Exod. 9:27; 10:8, 16), but ultimately his hard heart (9:7, 35) lost all pliability. God's hardening of Pharaoh's heart (10:20) confirmed what the Egyptian indicated he wanted all along, and God's earlier promise (see 3:19–20) came to pass.

All fall short of God's glory (Rom. 3:23), and the wages of sin is death (Rom. 6:23)—these too are promises of God, delivered by Paul, assuring destruction for those who adamantly turn from God's mercy. As is consistently the case, however, justice is tempered by mercy. Note the second part of Romans 6:23, where Paul says that "the gift of God is eternal life in Christ Jesus our Lord." Those who take advantage of this promised gift will be able, according to the Gospel, to miss the consequences of the more strident predictions. Still, the timetable is not given, so while there is the possibility of turning off a treacherous course, it is the Lord's prerogative to decide when clemency has reached its end in each particular case.

Through repeated exposure to Jesus' person and work, Judas is confronted with the love, grace, and expectations of God. Like any other, he can accept all this for himself and welcome God's entrance in his life and assistance for living to God's glory. Or he can resist. God responds to resistance in different ways. He persists, insisting on his love and interest, wooing like Cyrano outside Roxanne's window, promising affection to one barely cognizant of his presence. He overwhelms, pounding Jonah with a storm, blinding Paul with his light. He abandons, too. That he offers love to sinful rebels at all is breathtaking; he does not obligate himself to an infinite openness.

Judas is doomed to destruction because he consciously entertained the promptings of Satan (John 13:2) and resisted the embrace of a merciful God; he faces the same destiny as all who reject God. We think Judas to stand at the nadir of rebellion, that he is the best example of opposition to God. That is not the case: Scripture does not harp on any single standout example of human rebellion. In fact, after the brief, early mention of Judas in Acts, he is never heard of again in the New Testament. The point is this: Every person carries within what Judas—and others like him before and after—demonstrated. Think of others besides Judas "on the night [Jesus] was betrayed"

(1 Cor. 11:23): the religious leaders who were laying plans for Jesus' capture, or the crowd swelling Jerusalem that would refuse to protest when the One they had earlier called Lord and Teacher was dragged away by soldiers. On that night, traitors were everywhere, even in Jesus' inner circle.[4]

Shortly after dinner, Jesus and the Eleven removed to a garden on Mount Olivet. There he prayed, and then soldiers led by Judas came. Some at least among the Eleven stood to fight. Certainly Peter was there, but he quickly lost heart and hightailed it off the mountain. Jesus had predicted that Peter would act just this way. "I won't," he sputtered. "You will," Jesus promised. Another victim of predestination, or a man overwhelmed by circumstance and cowardice?

Having betrayed Jesus in Gethsemane, Peter crept into the high priest's courtyard where Jesus had been taken. There he strained for news, a look, exoneration. He fell again when a servant girl asked, "Aren't you with that guy they just brought in?" "No," insisted Peter not once but three times, vehemently, profanely, expertly convincing all but himself that Jesus and he were not comrades. John says Jesus caught Peter's eye at one point later that night; it was sufficient to reduce Peter to inconsolable sobbing.

Peter's story does not end with his sellout. Like Judas, he had taken a clear stand against Jesus. Both had capitulated when there was opportunity to support him. Both voiced strong objections to association with him; both insisted they were not part of his tribe. Both ran away; both experienced deep remorse. Both had opportunity to recant. But only one is restored. Why?

54

Peter's case is documented in John's Gospel. There we find this apostle back with the others after the frightful episodes of Jesus' arrest, trial, and death. Fishing early one morning, he heard the Lord call from the beach. Joyful, Peter dove overboard, sloshed inland, and fell at Jesus' feet. Humbled, he pledged his loyalty and resumed a life of submission to the Lord. Acts picks up the story, breathlessly following a revitalized Peter who presses on and never looks back.

And Judas? The records are less complete. Matthew 27 says that Judas, "seized with remorse" (v. 3), went back to the authorities. "I have sinned," he admitted, "for I have betrayed innocent blood" (v. 4). Was he looking for pardon? The priests and elders refused to give it, and Judas left, throwing the blood money at them in the Temple (v. 5). He then hung himself (v. 5) and so went to the place "where he belongs" (Acts 1:25). Whether he had another encounter with mercy or his heart was finally hardened is unclear.[5]

We hear often that we should not purposely put ourselves in harm's way or otherwise taunt God simply to see if he really will pull us through. But doesn't Jesus' invitation for Judas to join his camp sound perilously close to such a dare? Here is the difference: Jesus came into the world to save sinners. He could not accomplish this mission if he hung only with the well; he had to traffic among the sick. This meant that he was required to seek out those like Judas who held within themselves the potential for betrayal. Simply put, there were no other kinds of people to meet. Jesus' invitation for Judas to come and follow and his ongoing willingness to include Judas among the company of disciples did not signal a lapse of insight. His attitude pictures mercy's broad reach. This isn't a simple story at all.

Before betrayal is possible, a relationship must exist: The traitor sells out her country's secrets; the lover jilts his beloved. Betrayal is possible only once trust is given, making it an intense, emotional experience. When we open ourselves to another and make ourselves vulnerable, we expose ourselves to the possibility of being savaged. No one can tear a heart like a friend.

"Friend, do what you came for." Matthew remembers that Jesus said this to Judas (26:50), a point all the more poignant since earlier that same evening Matthew would also have heard Jesus describe the disciples as friends for whom he would lay down his life (John 15:13–15). What registered on Jesus' face as he spoke to Judas? What was swirling in his heart? To know that he would soon give his life for one such as this—it boggles the mind.

We scramble for an explanation. Some speculate that Judas's dastardly act came because he felt *he* had been betrayed—that Jesus had not made good on promises issued earlier in the game. On such a reading, Judas was either trying to provoke action from Jesus or responding out of spite for his lack of initiative. It's possible that Judas could no longer stand the high standards of Jesus.[6] The New Testament is surprisingly, maddeningly silent as to his motives, giving us only his actions. One leaves, one stays, both die. Only one death is constructive.

Jesus enters the room, reclines at table, and is aware of what is unfolding. He eats anyway. "I have eagerly anticipated this time together," he says, a sentiment echoed later by the author of Hebrews. In that book we're told that Jesus endured the cross "for the joy set before him" (12:2). How does one go to a cross with joy? Why would one be eager to eat with another intent on his demise? For Jesus, it gets back to love.[7]

Love is a matter of seeking out and staying with. Having come to a dark world in search of needy people, Jesus remains true to the end (see John 13:1). His love is pushed to the limit, stretched on the rack of human deceit, poured out indiscriminately. We say that God's love is unconditional, and it is, but we see here that it is also expressed without regard for consequence: Jesus does not do this to force a change in others. Devoid of manipulation, God's love is pure.

Ironically, what happens at this table requires the cross. An assassin might have slipped a stealthy knife into Jesus' heart, but this betrayal is a loud, unruly affair. Crucifixion's violence matches it and protests mightily against the crime of rebellion that only the cross can cover and redeem. Jesus did not die for us because we were bruised, but because we were completely rotten, spoiled through to the core. An extreme solution was necessary because an extreme condition had developed.

Here is the crowning ignominy: We are little different from those others who betrayed him. True, we quickly dismiss the religious professionals as boors and the crowds as buffoons, we easily rebuff Peter for his weakness, and we shudder at Judas's unthinkable treachery—but we are traitors, too. Consider: When we choose another over him, preferring the company of one less holy or the pleasures of an immediate gratification, is this not a slap in the face of a Friend—have we not broken our word of fidelity? What more is betrayal than that?

We look at Judas and are repulsed. He should have listened, we think, should have turned back to the Lord. Why risk the wrath of God? But we must also admit how often we carry in our hearts what he also bore. As we approach the Eucharist, it must be with the full knowledge of our proclivity toward rebellion. Like others that night, we who have heard the gospel often turn faster than a figure skater, and we will turn again. This is why we must eat and drink repeatedly, to wash throats inclined to promise allegiance to one other than the Lord, to hit bellies otherwise enticed by the favors of idols.

The dark night of betrayal cannot muffle the strong chords of mercy or dim the bright light of judgment as real and potential traitors stand before their intended victim. He holds out the bread and cup as to friends. He sees into hearts and extends forgiveness. He evokes a rush of remorse, or a hardening; loyalty will be compromised or renewed at this table.

Four

This Loaf, This Cup

In the Garden, the Lord walked with Adam and Eve in the cool of the day. One time when he went there expecting the company of these two, God found them missing, hiding from him, unwilling to admit their recent disobedience. The sin that yielded shame damaged their close relationship and severed fellowship between God and his people.

In the wilderness, the Lord gave Moses plans for a tabernacle where his presence would dwell. This elaborate portable structure took months to build and once completed occupied a place of pride among Jacob's traveling children. Any person moving through the camp would have noticed this tabernacle; its central location, its sheer size, and that hovering pillar of cloud or fire above it drew attention, reminding people that God was in their midst.

In the time of the judges and during the reign of kings, the relationship between God and his people oscillated; often prophets delivered messages from God's heart about the desire for closeness and the reality of infidelity. Through Isaiah, God promised Immanuel, who would come to live with those he loved. *Immanuel,* as Matthew later explains when he deals with the birth of Jesus, means *God is with us* (1:23).

In Capernaum, Jesus stood among the people, teaching about the nature of God. He had come to this new "hometown" once Nazareth had rejected him. Speaking to a crowd a short time before the Feast of Tabernacles—a time when Israel commemorated their pilgrimage through that wilderness and God's resplendent promise to dwell more permanently among his people—Jesus gave one of his most scandalous lessons. "I am the bread of life," he declared, ". . . bread that comes down from heaven, which a man may eat and not die. . . . I tell you the truth, unless you eat the flesh of the Son of Man and drink his blood, you have no life in you" (John 6:35, 50, 53).[1] Twenty centuries later you can still hear the gasp. Jesus' first listeners were shocked; subsequent interpreters have scurried to slap a metaphorical collar on these words to make them safe for other readers. But in focusing on ways to dodge the bullet of cannibalism, we miss the target for which Jesus was aiming. In this discourse, Jesus is repeating what God has been demonstrating since humanity appeared on earth's stage: God longs to dwell among people.

"He who comes to me will never go hungry, and he who believes in me will never be thirsty," Jesus says (John 6:35), emphasizing not the sating of appetite but the desire for proximity. "Whoever comes to me I will never drive away" (6:37); "whoever eats my flesh and drinks my blood remains in me" (6:56). The scandal here is not that Jesus nudges people toward the unthinkable ingestion of human flesh but rather that the holy, pure, and perfect God would want a relationship with sulky, uneven, small-minded people.

This relationship depends on amelioration of the sin that originally disrupted fellowship and on response from those sought by God—the willingness on their part to turn toward him and say yes. When Jesus refers to his body and blood,[2] he is taking up the first of these requirements, announcing the incredibly good, totally unexpected news that sin will be paid for by means of the sacrifice he intends to make. When Jesus calls people to "eat" and "drink" (as in 6:56), he is explaining that those called by God, those drawn to him (see 6:44), can and must take him into themselves. There is a conscious act of reception and follow-through, much as one who receives an invitation to a party must show up at the appointed time and place in order to dance.

It is possible, as some commentators have observed, that John includes this episode as his take on the Last Supper. But what if instead Jesus has stepped here into a stream that had been coursing for centuries already and is referring again to the central core of the prophetic message he had come to deliver: that people facing condemnation for their sin need what Jesus will make available by his sacrifice so that they can enjoy unbroken fellowship with God. How fitting that he does this during Passover, a festival that had been designed to impress that central truth deep into human hearts.

As a "member of the clergy," I was invited to a local school's graduation ceremony to pray. I accepted on account of a belief that it is important to bring God into

61

situations like this—or rather that it is good to bring God *back* to such events.

The educational system which most strongly influences this school is based on the view that God values learning and ought to be part of one's intellectual development. As U.S. history indicates, the first schools of the nation were founded by religious people who saw God as integral to life. That viewpoint has since been challenged, and current educational theory deals little with God as a direct influence, but some early traits linger: many schools still have clergy come to pray at graduation.

The biblical record indicates that Passover had suffered a similar fate: A holy time for commemorating God's miraculous activity had, over the years, become a simple holiday where God showed up more like a candle than a bonfire. It is certainly true that people in our day routinely keep holidays with little concern as to their religious underpinnings—Christmas is a prime example. Something very like this had happened with Passover, so when Jesus gathered his disciples for the meal, he peeled back layers of ceremony to expose God's lavish grace pouring out on impoverished toddlers, adolescents, and adults. Passover's checkered history of celebration and neglect had fostered a sense of benign indifference toward deeper matters. It had become another "special date" for the calendar, another day or few days off from the normal routine. Surely for some it retained its true power, but by and large Passover had not penetrated hearts. As the religious leaders of Jesus' day illustrated repeatedly, the glorious celebrations of God's miraculous activity no longer evoked repentance, obedience, or worship; these days perfunctory people had many rules to obey and enforce but lacked the warmth of a life-changing relationship with the Lord. For them, God had become a concept, a principle, a custom. The power and mercy on display when lambs' blood first ran down doorframes had faded from active memory.

So Jesus plunges in, stripping away the debris accumulated over years of neglect and indifference. Rather than emphasizing an accurate reading of history or insisting on the "right way of doing Passover," he focuses on why Passover happened at all. He emphasizes the need for sacrifice to save a people captured and captivated by sin. He reminds them that even whiners were precious to God and warranted rescue. He speaks about the means of that rescue: not the ritual slaying of an innocent lamb but the violent sacrifice of himself. He looks ahead to a joyful reunion when God can finally and fully be with his people.

In the upper room, Jesus takes the bread: "This is my body, which is for you." Then he holds the cup: "This cup is the new covenant in my blood" (1 Cor. 11:24–25). Scholarly and denominational discussions of this meal and its significance ponder the meaning of *is:* does one interpret this literally, such that the bread and wine truly are Jesus' flesh and blood,[3] or is it a more figurative meaning he has in mind?[4] But pull back a bit further, away from questions of grammar or style, and listen to what he is saying. What if Jesus is after those hearts tilting toward the grand and good? For months he has been insisting that God is on the move. Now he sits with bread and cup, ready once more to rehearse his central speech about sin, sacrifice, and fellowship. If we set aside *this* and *is* for a moment, we will be better able to hear the rest of his words.

Like *given*. Jesus is about to be torn—by thorn and spear—like a loaf shredded for distribution among diners. Jesus readies bread so that it can be given; by grace, his body will also be surrendered. Had he remained intact—that is, unwilling to share himself with others—sin's penalty would have run unchecked among humanity. As it is, "the grace of God that brings salvation has appeared to all" (Titus 2:11) precisely because Jesus was willing to give himself completely.[5]

One of our daughters dances, and she regales us with stories that help me understand Jesus' generosity in a fresh way. In the world of ballet it is an accepted fact that dancing is costly. To succeed at the craft demands countless hours, as well as a great deal of footwear. Toe shoes, for example, essential for dancing *en pointe*, hardly last. Taken new from the box, they are pummeled mercilessly, bent and strained by use, discarded and replaced. These shoes resemble a dancer's body, which will be similarly abused. To dance ballet, one will leap and land many times, and in the process jar a spine unaccustomed to and not designed for such purposes. This is why few dancers last more than a decade at the professional level; most have severely damaged vertebrae by then. Still, they dance. They dance to satisfy an inner muse and later a demanding audience; they dance in response to an urge to craft a work of beauty. In the process, they destroy the very body given over to this purpose. Jesus too was propelled into his ministry by the desire to do something beautiful, something good. His success resulted in the blessing of many; it also exacted a terrible toll.

We'll also notice *for you*. Jesus is pointing out the wonderful reality that the grim work of the cross awaiting him is done for the benefit of others. "You need what

I am about to give," he says. "While the world may set itself against you, always keep firmly in mind that I am for you, that I want to be with you." As bread and wine when eaten and drunk become part of a person, so the Lord seeks such intimacy with his people; God's own are held very close. Jesus' words indicate that God is making fellowship possible.

Third, we'll catch Paul's "explanation" of the cup as "the new covenant in my blood." Necessary because older covenants had been broken[6] and new because God's work among people is more progressive than static,[7] this covenant is like previous agreements where God promises certain benefits to those willing to agree with and implement his directions. Like all covenants, this new one has a physical—and sacrificial—component: blood flows at its institution. The remarkable development with this covenant is that it is Jesus' blood.

A reference to covenant moves us across theological terrain where many roads have been cleared and many way stations built. It is enough for our purposes here to recall that the language of covenant, when used by God, is ancient and integral to the human story. Covenants date back to Abraham, Noah, and even Adam; they indicate God's promises of commitment to people (he is *for* them early on!) and call forth from them allegiance and obedience. That invitation requires a choice, and with this choice come implications for subsequent life and the promise of blessing.

The new covenant, like those that preceded it, provided the terms under which God's people would now relate to him but did not disparage what had come before. Earlier promises were still remembered; they described the Lord's intentions and hopes, and they proved his faithfulness. In this latest installment, all that God had been leading up to would now be fulfilled[8]—until such time as God was ready for the *next* piece of his plan. The covenant Jesus announced resembled what was already familiar: It was initiated by God, offered because of need, accompanied by promises of blessing, and delivered with an expectation of behavior from its recipients. Like all others before it, this one was instituted with sacrifice.

What is "new" about this covenant? God's widened interest in "all people everywhere" (1 Cor. 1:2) and his gracious provision of a payment plan that is not temporary or partial but eternal and total. The way in which this covenant is established is also new. Like every previous covenant, this one is sealed with blood—but not the blood of an animal. Jesus, taking the cup, says the blood will be his own. It is a radical departure not only from the Passover script but from the way in which covenants have operated to this point. No bird nor lamb nor bull will suffice for this new covenant. Jesus' blood alone will seal it; his life will be the sacrifice. "The Son of Man did not come to be served, but to serve," Jesus had said and now demonstrated this night by washing feet. "And," he had added, "to give his life as a ransom for many" (Mark 10:45). That prediction was coming true as his disciples watched: the "pouring out" of this sacrifice was nearly complete.[9]

Jesus lifts only two items from a table otherwise resplendent with food and drink and, with hands that will soon be pinned to a cross, breaks bread and passes wine. Those that hold these "elements" today know their simplicity and their power; they know that *element* is an apt description—for bread and wine, so basic, form building blocks for life.

As I stand before a congregation about to break bread together, at times—often—I am nearly overcome. I was raised to view the things on this table as "symbols," but there is a power here and a weight that pulls me deeper. The bread and cup act like prisms so that as I look at them, I see much more emerge. I am struck by time: as bread and wine require the passing of time, so Jesus arrived at "just the right time." I feel the flour rough and dry on my hands as I tear the loaf; it will linger long after I have consumed a morsel. Those ingredients speak, too, of variety, integrity, chemistry. I catch a glint from the surface of violet, violent liquid. If I bump the cup, its contents will spill and stain, as stubbornly as blood, the cloth beneath. I recall that wine comes only after crushing—as is the case with flour, so important for bread.[10] Portions pass among communicants, small as samples in a grocery store, whetting our appetites for more of what God has for us.

Bread and wine help Jesus bring God back into the picture, as Passover was supposed to do. But notice: He is not simply interested in helping these twelve men be successful in "doing" Passover. He uses that occasion to press a deeper point, taking disciples into the realm of a God who has long been addressing in various ways people with whom he desires a relationship. He wants to live close in—remember that tabernacle and the pillar of cloud or fire in the very middle of the camp?—and to have people consumed by him; he will do whatever is necessary to see that come about. He will pour himself out like a drink, will gladly suffer tearing so that all might have a piece. He will give all of himself to these people, if only they will welcome him into their very lives.

Five

He Gave Thanks

Before Jesus passed food around to those who despite professions of faith still had divided hearts, he paused to give thanks. The Gospel writers had alerted us to Jesus' custom in this regard earlier, when describing his feeding of several thousand people. Then he had instructed the Twelve to organize a great throng in order to receive a meal that would start with five loaves and two fish. Taking these items and "looking up to heaven, he gave thanks and broke the loaves" (Matt. 14:19). The disciples passed this food among many; "all ate and were satisfied," and later, after a sweep of the crowd, the disciples managed to find an additional twelve baskets of leftovers (Matt. 14:20). Jesus had been feeding this gang all day with his teaching, and the nourishing continued as they sat down for dinner. But before everyone ate, he gave thanks.

So it is at that final supper with his disciples. Jesus has for years been feeding these friends with teaching designed to nourish their souls. He will speak again in this upper room, will serve, will pray. Then he will break bread to pass among those who must eat, knowing that soon these same men will abandon him, or worse—and that in a few hours he himself will be carted off to face those who will gleefully condemn him to death. So when he pauses to pray, what is happening?

Give thanks in all circumstances. This advice from Paul to his friends in Thessalonica (1 Thess. 5:18) is abrupt, lofty, and a tad dispiriting. Smoothing it with another translation or paraphrase won't help much; knowledge of the original Greek hardly softens its impact. Paul counsels thankfulness no matter what is wrapping around your ankles or boring into your eyebrows. He sounds unrealistic here, quixotic, attempting to launch both the ancients and us on some impossible dream. A life of thankfulness *sounds* good, no doubt, but it is hard-pressed by reality. After all, circumstances require attention, and so many leave little space for giving thanks. When the rain falls and the roof leaks, one doesn't pause to glory in the discomfort but gathers buckets, hammers, nails, and shingles. When the hacking cough won't subside, when the stock market stays depressed, when the kid is failing algebra and buying weird CDs, when the stars are out and you're still at the office—where does thankfulness fit?

Here is where it takes faith to read the Bible. Because when you go to Scripture with an ear open for what it might just possibly have to say to your complex existence, you're likely to be surprised or perplexed. You may well conclude that those people back then didn't really face what looms before you now, that the days they woke to were smog-free and full of birdsong and that their children were perfect, their "good" cholesterol counts high, their relationships uncomplicated, and their mailboxes, answering machines, and e-mail accounts blissfully uncluttered—in short that what the Bible dealt with back then hardly resembles the smallest slice of the life in which you are now immersed. It takes faith to read the Bible and to believe that what you find there might light fires that illumine your brain, warm your heart, and cook up something that you'd find satisfying and good.

Take Job. We read the story about this prosperous, highly-regarded, devoted family man and how after rapid, concussive blows, he lost everything. Curse God and die, counseled his wife. Instead, Job falls to the ground in worship. "The LORD gave and the LORD has taken away," he says, "may the name of the LORD be praised" (Job 1:20–21). We think, *Could I thank God in the face of so much disaster?*

Then there is the story in Luke 17 about ten men afflicted with leprosy, a disease that attacked personal comfort and obliterated social status. Jesus met these lepers one day and, hearing their piteous cries, sent them to the local priests—the ones responsible for judging them fit to reenter the community. On the way, each man discovered that he had been healed. One came back to Jesus. He threw himself down before Jesus and, "praising God," let thanks pour out of his mouth in the loud voice that had earlier begged for mercy. But Jesus is not satisfied. "Were not all ten cleansed?" he asks. "Where are the other nine? Was no one found to return and give praise to God except this foreigner?" (Luke 17:17).

Both stories blow up in our face. Given Job's setbacks, we'd understand a little grousing. We sympathize with the lepers, too—they'd been out of work and out of touch, and now a little partying was surely called for. But in each case we'd be wrong. Both returning leper and local lord show us that God wants his people to be thankful folk, ready to praise him rain or shine. Each of these characters recognizes what comes as from the hand of God; both fall at his feet in gratitude. They show us that circumstances should not distract us from giving thanks but rather serve as reminders for what people of faith are supposed to engage in. Notice the last part of 1 Thessalonians 5:18: Paul says there that giving thanks is "God's will." Thanks-giving in the midst of life is commanded and expected, but it is also a result. It emerges from those who recognize God's activity, from those being formed and re-formed by the Lord. Like Paul says in another letter, we who have been graced by God's salvation exist to praise—a large part of which involves thanks—God.[1] In other words, the apostle is telling us who are supposed to be living in line with the will of God that a life characterized by thanks-giving is precisely what our Lord desires and precisely what our Lord, on the night he was betrayed, demonstrates.

As our kids moved into the verbal stage, we began to add a few more guidelines to family life together. We directed them, for instance, to say "please" and "thank you." We had our reasons for this, of course. We wanted our kids to be polite and well-mannered; we wanted our own reputations to survive their toddler years. We also hoped to teach some theology early on. For to say "thank you" sincerely means stepping outside oneself to acknowledge that another can—or must—provide what is needed. Taking and grasping, assuming oneself competent and sufficient, and justifying acquisitions as one's right is another option—and one commonly chosen by those we call "spoiled"—but those who walk through life refusing to say thanks gradually shrivel.

Gratitude makes life plump and full. Picture Nehemiah's triumphant conclusion to the extraordinary building project he directed. For weeks the people have been furtive and fearful, sniped at by nearby enemies. Then, when the last brick is laid, Nehemiah gathers the entire community for a celebration. He shatters the bunker mentality by sending the city's leaders to the top of the wall, and then priests and musicians. A choir of singers, divided in two, follows, each group leading people in opposite directions around the wall. As they go, they are singing their thanks to God so that "the sound of rejoicing in Jerusalem could be heard far away" (Neh. 12:27–43).

The Psalms provide a libretto for choirs like these. Give thanks to the Lord, for he is good, they say repeatedly (Psalms 106, 107, 118, and 136 are examples), urging us to notice God's goodness no matter what, widening us with appeals to God's grace. Praise gushes like waterfalls, tumbling, roaring, enchanting, exposing us to both those who provide and those who themselves have need. Thanks break triumphantly over treacherous reefs and flow through us to God, the originator of "every good and perfect gift" (James 1:17).

"While they were eating, Jesus took bread, gave thanks and broke it. . . . Then he took the cup, gave thanks and offered it to them" (Matthew 26:26–27). Each Synoptic Gospel describes Jesus' experience with the Twelve around a table just hours before his arrest in the garden, and each repeats that twice Jesus "gave thanks." Two

Greek verbs appear; of these the more frequent is *eu-charistō*.[2] With English letters, this becomes *eucharist*, one of the ways the church refers to this celebration. The verb itself is a compound word, built with the prefix *eu*, for *good*, and the noun *charis*, for *grace*. To speak, then, of communion with this word is to call attention to the demands and implications of thanks-giving when one is confronted by the goodness of grace. *Eucharist* takes us outside ourselves, exposing both our need and our pride.

We do not easily give thanks, because we quite readily imagine ourselves to be competent, capable, and in control. To whom other than ourselves should we be grateful? We can buy what we need and use what we buy with little thought as to where it came from. What surrounds us is our doing, we surmise, here because I found or earned or paid for it. So when I read, mow, drive, or eat, I am simply enjoying the fruit of my labors. All this is mine, brought close by my industry and cleverness. Right?

And yet Jesus gives thanks. Maybe it was an expression of good manners; maybe it was more than that. Consider the deep theology of thanks-giving: I give thanks, offered with sincerity and thoughtfulness, upon recognition that what I have has come from another familiar with my wants and needs. Despite an appearance of independence, I am a consumer far more than a producer—and there are needs I cannot meet by myself. Can I admit that? And am I interested in the source from which what I need flows? And will I be grateful for what comes?

Gratitude wells up within us occasionally, and we direct it at a parent, spouse, friend, child, boss, or rock star.

But there is a more basic source for what we have and a better target for our thankfulness. This is what Jesus demonstrates, when he pauses to "give thanks" before passing bread and cup. He acknowledges the gracious provision of God and once more sets an example for his followers. In every aspect of your life, Jesus would say, there is opportunity to give thanks. Start with what's easy, basic—like meals. Before you "break bread," give thanks. Allow every meal to be sacramental, where physical matter provokes spiritual reflection.

According to Luke, believers met often to "break bread" (see Acts 2:42, 46; 20:7). Debate arises over the precise nature of these meals: were they formal "communion services" or more casual potlucks? In some respects, it hardly matters; it is wonderful to have evidence that Christians enjoyed being together enough to share food and easy enough to imagine that when they gathered, talk would have turned to their Lord. On the other hand, it's probably significant that Luke describes this action with a phrase found in each account of Jesus' last meal. Luke may be giving us another insight into early community life, showing us further occasions when believers would have consciously responded like the psalmists to evidence of God's goodness. For Christians, the presence of food indicates God's faithful provision, and the step to a "eucharist," a thanking of our good and gracious God, would be readily prompted by this circumstance.

But it's easy to get distracted. Families eat together around a table less often, or they rush to consume the vittles or watch TV over their chicken and biscuits. Responsibilities queue up outside the door and food can be

75

effortlessly phoned in or picked up; few meals occasion special notice. Does giving thanks fit with this scene? Do we come to our food ravenous, or bored—or can we approach the table, no matter what edibles it offers, with a certain reverence? It is likely that we will bring to the Lord's Supper an attitude similar to the one we have for those other suppers in homes or restaurants. So perhaps it is high time to slow the gallop to a canter, or even a walk, and lean down to smell roses on that trail. Grace spreads like a cloth over this table, and the cross's shadow is playing over the elements; it's enough to melt our hearts in the glow of God's goodness so that they bubble with praise. Hard people like us can crawl out from beneath circumstances to find in communion exactly what we need and, like Jesus and his disciples, give thanks.[3]

From time to time Sue and I visit the home of mentors we've known for two decades. Both of these friends are near 70 and maintain a pace that would make younger folk quail. They have been disciples for years, and each comes from a family steeped in Christian tradition. During our last stay with them, I was caught by the way they prayed before our meals together. If there are those for whom this exercise might have become rote or for whom lapses might be forgiven, one might expect that these would be the people. But instead their mealtime prayers afforded fresh occasions to remember the Lord, bring before him absent friends and family, and express gratitude for present grace and mercy. Those prayers seasoned the food and conversation that followed and set among us an aura that only enhanced the fellowship of a meal.

Circumstances are prompts for giving thanks. They come not to run life but as part of it. That means that sickness or health, tranquility or upheaval, wealth or poverty, or the innumerable states in between can lead one to thanks-giving rather than make one stray from it. Meals serve as wonderful entry points for adopting or honing this practice. Why not consciously invite the Lord as a guest at our table or use the opportunity to bow before him in gratitude, to recognize him at the outset of what is so necessary and enjoyable? Giving thanks verbalizes the flow of grace. At meals, we notice that what lies on this table, what sustains our life routinely, is not of our own doing; we have had help. So we pause to affirm that there is Another who knows us, loves us, and provides for us—One who understands our needs and commits to meeting them. This generous provider routinely goes beyond meeting needs to bless us in ways that delight and encourage us. To this One we freely, gladly give thanks.

As we do, Jesus' example at the Supper comes to mind. Here is One who, despite all that is swirling around him, regardless of what is about to come crashing down on him, pauses to look up and say "thank you." From this simple act the entire service gets its name, *Eucharist*, when all who follow the Lord themselves pause to express their gratitude—for the food he gives, for the life he makes possible, and for the good grace of God so richly bestowed.[4]

Two of Jesus' disciples, badly shaken by recent events, were walking to a little village south of Jerusalem. In the city that had been so blessed by God's hand, God's Son had just days before been killed. A stranger joined the pair and talked with them about what had happened. He seemed unaware of the tragedy, unfamiliar with the news that "a prophet, powerful in word and deed" (Luke 24:19) had been crucified. "Some of our own folk," these two told their new companion, "went to the tomb only to hear—from angels, no less!—that this same prophet was alive. But others who went to check found no trace of him." And so their sad walk—away from Jerusalem—continued.

Then the stranger began to speak, explaining from Scripture what was true "concerning himself" (Luke 24:27). The stranger, of course, is Jesus, and as he tells this story (in Luke 24:13–35) Luke is tugging at the testimony of those who claim faith in him. "How foolish you are, and how slow of heart to believe!" (v. 25). Luke records these words of the Lord as an indictment of all who profess allegiance but for whom circumstance overwhelms faith. But there is more than criticism. The two walkers pull into their destination, and Jesus acts as though he will press on. They implore him to stay, apparently intrigued by his mastery of the Scriptures related to the one they followed, and perhaps also by his forthright manner. He agrees, and they go inside to eat.

Then this: "When he was at the table with them, he took bread, gave thanks, broke it and began to give it to them. Then their eyes were opened and they recognized him" (v. 30–31). What tipped them off? They tell others the story later on, and Luke understands that the lights went on "when he broke the bread" (v. 35). Before passing the bread to be eaten, it had to be broken, and before Jesus tore the loaf, he gave thanks. This thanks was his regular custom, whether he was with several thousand or with two. Can you imagine hearing his voice? Did he quote a psalm or speak extemporaneously? Or did he, perhaps, just say "grace"?

Here's what nearly got lost beneath the blistering circumstances surrounding the crucifixion: the goodness of God. To many, Jesus' death was overwhelming, dominant; it could easily have knocked them off balance. When Jesus appears to a few and then breaks bread with them, there is a sudden flash of insight. The light goes on: the Lord *is* good. Thank God.

Six

Remember

Both Paul and Luke include a word from Jesus about remembering in their accounts of the Last Supper. It surprises, in a way: Could one ever forget Jesus? The passionate way he handled God's Word, the empathy with which he dealt with people, the force with which he met the hypocrisy of religious leaders, the tenderness he had for the poor and distressed—surely these would have made an indelible impression. The problem is that we *do* forget. We have minds that decay, and data, even precious information, drops out. Or our brains overload, and one experience is soon replaced by another, more recent and vivid. One person, even an important, significant person, can be nearly overwritten, like on a computer disk or chalkboard. That teacher, friend, boss, pastor, neighbor, teammate with whom you were once so close—does that person linger in your mind, or only put in a guest appearance from time to time? Or sometimes we simply turn away and occupy ourselves with something else.

Jesus knows these tendencies, and since he wants to stay fresh in the minds of his followers so that their hearts will stay soft to his ways, he leaves some appropriate mementos.

"Can a mother forget the baby at her breast and have no compassion on the child she has borne?" God asks this of people bent on walking away from him. "Though she may forget, I will not forget you" (Isa. 49:15). It's a promise from the Lord, given to build our confidence. Sadly, we don't keep this promise in our "active" file. He may always have us in mind, but we forget him.

We forget because we're human and as humans our capacity to remember shrinks over time. This is painfully obvious in my own experience: As time goes by, more and more drops out of my memory banks. Who was my third grade gym teacher? Don't know. How was it I spent the summer of 1972? Hmmm. Where did I put that silver dollar my great-grandmother gave me? Other, more important details grow fuzzier by the day.

Some people forget more slowly. My sister, for instance, can recall sights, activities, and events with amazing clarity (although, as I tell her, if she's the only one who remembers, how can the rest of us prove her wrong?). My wife can rattle off the menu from a dinner party ten years ago. My friend can list minor league baseball players who vaulted to the bigs. But for me, memory is spotty at best. True, my mind holds some trivia, like the names of supporting actors in B-movies. But this hardly counts. And what is distressing is that things I ought to know, matters I want to keep close at hand—these slip away like shuffleboard disks across the tiles of my neural pathways. I should remember, for instance, to be compassionate, consistent, and careful.

Sometimes "normal" failings are hustled along by disease. For example, Alzheimer's assaults one's memory and leaves one without anchors. Alzheimer's produces a kind of mental vertigo, cutting one loose from firm footings so that its victims feel nearly helpless, lost and afraid. As with vertigo, when a person must become still and wait for the room to stop spinning, this illness leaves one without a dependable balance, unmoored and inactive. Lacking memory, the ability to navigate time and space disintegrates. It's exasperating, frightening, debilitating, and even humiliating for those suffering and for those close to them. It is also a painful reminder of how we run down and what slows or stops when we do.

We forget because we so easily fill our minds with other things, too. We leave off training ourselves to remember; we peel away the little notes and pictures that speak of God's goodness and coat the wall with fresh paint. We stop talking about God, start watching more TV, find reasons to stay away from church, take up new hobbies. The badge of busyness we wear so proudly grows larger and heavier and shinier, very quickly filling the mirrors we consult with the flashy reflections of bright lights that dazzle us. "You have forsaken your first love" (Rev. 2:4), the Lord says to the church at Ephesus, a group that had flourished under Paul's encouragement and then languished. Their ancient problem has a familiar ring.

There is another, more specious reason we forget. Dissatisfaction with the Lord, evidenced by active rebellion or the more subtle acquisition of idols in various forms, erodes our ability—and desire—to remember him. We find something more appealing, less demanding, and think *This is what I'm after.* We become so enamored, our minds so occupied, that we let go of God. I've watched people enticed by the prospect of a new or better job or relationship cut their ties and move into a situation that promises to be a great improvement. "What will this mean for your spiritual development?" I ask, particularly of those who finally seem to be growing again after a long dormancy. "I'll be okay," they declare, "and besides, this is such a good opportunity." They leave and plunge into this new thing, and later when I ask I hear that, well, there hasn't really been as much time as we'd like for God or his church, and sure, I'm gonna do better with my disciplines, and no, we really haven't found friends who encourage our faith. But we will. And besides, this is such a great opportunity.

Remember. It's a leading word, a combination of a prefix that stresses repetition and a noun that emphasizes one part of a whole. When I re-member, I come back together with something I had left; once more I am joined to the larger body of events or people. My self would prefer to be alone or to have all around me serve my interests, so I need to re-member, to re-up, to join afresh. My culture would have me insulate myself from others, so I need to re-turn, re-group.

Remembering keeps us linked with the group of which we ought to be part. It also helps us function as we should. This is one of memory's important roles, offering assistance with tasks both mundane and critical. Normal memory keeps us on track with conversation, responsibilities, and routine maintenance. When it slips, we experience difficulty in staying linked with a community; the loss of memory tends to isolate.

The technology sector seems to be discovering almost daily increasingly impressive ways of capturing and keeping data with an array of "memory storage devices." We can buy these, and like toasters they are meant to improve the quality of our lives. But often they only allow us more quantity. We still forget so much. We drop balls, neglect agendas, have brain cramps. Sometimes the hard drives fill up or hideously crash. Others understand and readily forgive, because they row in similar boats. "Me too," we say ruefully, crimping the phone to a shoulder while tapping at the keyboard and keeping an eye on the TV. The ability to remember is different from the desire; intentions are less important than action.

Remember. Jesus holds the bread and cup, looking at his disciples. He knows about busy lives, ailing minds, intense temptations to head elsewhere. He knows his followers are likely to forget, consciously or otherwise, what has happened, even what is about to occur. "Don't," he pleads. Keep it fresh in your minds and hearts; talk often about what the Lord has done in, for, around, and through you. "*This* will help," he suggests, raising the loaf, indicating the wine. Like pictures in an album or trinkets on a shelf, these will draw you in and keep your memory fresh.

By remembering Jesus, we recall his clear teaching and manifest love. As we do this, we also evaluate: In what ways does my life reflect the person and work of the Lord? Writing to the Corinthians about behavior during the celebration of communion, Paul calls for those assembled to "examine" themselves (1 Cor. 11:28). Originally, this direction was made to people having difficulty in properly "recognizing the body of the Lord" (11:29). Abusive tendencies had slipped into their practice of table fellowship, such that a holy act among the community had turned into a time of self-satisfaction. Wanting to correct this, Paul urged careful consideration of motive and heart.[1]

We come professing to be close friends but know deeper down that we are really more indifferent, or even actively opposed. The hypocrisy may not be evident, of course, particularly when we are well-dressed and well-coiffed and when we kneel, sit, or stand with others to receive the bread and cup. But there we are, women and men who in the course of the week or month or several months since our last meeting for this purpose have said to the Lord in various ways, no. This Lord is not ours; we have proved that by our actions, thoughts, and words. We come, however, out of habit, as deeply ingrained as a Jewish Passover. We are "in church," and when the elements are present, we plan to partake. Careful consideration of the Lord and our own loyalty to him is not an item on the agenda.

It should be. Paul's Corinthians had adopted so cavalier an attitude as to wolf down a meal before those truly needing one had opportunity to eat. They could look around smugly and think *I've come. I'm here. Let's get on with it.* Paul dams this swift river with the recollection of Jesus' instruction to remember and with his own demand: Examine yourself. Have you moved away from God lately? Do not take no for an answer.

When we lived in Costa Rica, my wife and I helped a new congregation get established at a beach community to the north. For two years we'd travel to meet with this group every few weeks. I preferred to drive the 200 miles, but when time was tight, we'd fly. The plane we used sat fourteen, including two pilots. By my reckoning that was at least 150 people too few. Small planes unnerve me; we seem perilously close to the outside, which, once we've taken off, is very high above solid earth. From my seat I could watch the pilots fly; I was close enough no matter where I sat to read nearly every gauge.

Most of the brief trip was over level ground. On either end, however, we passed over small mountain ranges. This unsettled the air, which unsettled the plane. And most disconcerting of all, the instrument panel emitted a loud beep when we were approaching these hills. As far as I could tell, this noise was meant to alert the pilots that there were mountains ahead. This seemed patently obvious to me simply by looking out the front window. And perhaps it was obvious to them as well. Of course, it may also have been that in the business of flying this plane, of attending to the many dials and details, they might lose focus for a moment. Or they might have become calloused to their job, figuring that with so many hours logged or so many repetitions of this trip, there was nothing new to see; they could relax. But to make sure these problems didn't occur, the dashboard blared, and I for one was glad of it. Having those pilots keenly focused and aware was important to me. I didn't want them assuming too much; I was interested in more than their good intentions.

Paul's warnings alert communicants to the seriousness of what lies before them. How easy to assume that having done this before, having been here so often, all will proceed as normal and nothing new needs consideration. Little wonder, then, with such an approach, that communicants can slip into an idleness that threatens community and an indifference that degrades the Lord.

Examine yourself. You may sit before this table with good intentions, ready to affirm your loyalty to the Lamb slain on your behalf. But how long ago were you provoked to anger? When did lust last have a slow dance in your mind? Has pride or envy moved into a spare room nearby? Has exuberance for the Lord cooled? Has enthusiasm for his Word waned?

As Margaret Clarkson's version of the classic hymn "Come, Thou Fount" puts it, we are "prone to wander." Songwriter Chris Rice updates the same idea:

> On the surface not a ripple
> Undercurrent wages war
> Quiet in the sanctuary
> Sin is crouching at my door
>
> How can I be so prone to wander
> So prone to leave You, so prone to die
> And how can You be so full of mercy
> You race to meet me and bring me back to life
>
> I wake to find my soul in fragments
> Given to a thousand loves
> But only One will have no rival
> Hangs to heal me, spills His blood . . .[2]

Remembering the Lord counters that propensity to wander; Paul's comment about examination has a similar effect. Might one's schedule have crowded Christ out? Might one's routine simply include a slot for church without pausing to bring in a heart soft to God's grace? What are we likely to find as we probe? Hearts more like mica than marble, fissured and cracked and easily divided. Our resolve to follow Christ and Christ alone melts when we are pressed, or hassled, or simply given a more appealing alternative. We betray him easily, and for so little.

Like the weather. In pastoring local churches I've had people tell me they didn't come to the service last week because of the snow. Or the sun. It was too nice to stay in or too lousy to head out. My part, I gather, is to smile and nod approval of this reasoning. Of course, I should say. I understand.

One denominational executive, writing for his group's magazine, was more understanding. He identified the ownership of vacation cabins "at the lake" or "in the woods" as a deterrent to congregational worship on Sundays and concluded that the church may as well accept that people will blow town on weekends. His solution? Have the church and its staff and leaders available for services at other times.

Church facilities that are "open for business" other than Sunday mornings is a fine idea, but not when motivated by an effort simply to make worship more convenient. Such logic carried further results in shorter times together and increasing segregation ("I didn't come because my neighbor was going and, you know, we're just not getting along these days . . ."). It reduces the pointed call to gather to a fuzzy hope that we'll share a little space sometime.

Push this further, recognizing that while "church" includes gathered worship, it is also more. What will stir us to accept a life of humble service, to endure prolonged illness, to give sacrificially of our accumulated wealth, to confront those who struggle, to speak for those unheard? None of these is comfortable or particularly advantageous; on the contrary, the way of Christ often means a ladder down. What could possibly lead us to pursue that?

Divided hearts won't bear the load. Betrayal falls out as the crack widens. So Paul calls for the re-membering that requires an examination. Note, though, that while he advocates a demanding course, he is not attempting to limit participation. The clear implication is that people will, once they have examined themselves, take part. Paul's interest is in rooting out those traitorous ways, not in excluding unworthy candidates. Neither would he lay an inordinate burden on prospective communicants. He wants people to come—but he urges that they come ready.

Readiness requires a soft heart and an environment conducive to quiet and careful examination. If the session that includes communion is so packed with tasks the leaders must complete and information they must convey, the time necessary will be hurried or unavailable. So we must take care on the front end of communion, preparing participants to probe, training them in confession, encouraging them to repent.

As I move through my days, flying or coasting or slogging uphill, my heart toughens under a welter of experiences and is calloused by harsh influences. It takes little imagination to realize the effect of classrooms or the marketplace on tender hearts. If I am a person who has consciously welcomed Jesus as Lord, my heart faces further challenges: His lordship is routinely questioned by what I encounter.

For some, these experiences are sufficient to warrant a move far from detrimental influence and the creation of alternate societies or environments. This can enjoy some limited success but suffers from at least two difficulties. On the one hand, when I step away from one community, that group no longer has the benefit of my presence. As a follower of Jesus tasked with leavening my surroundings, I must somehow reconcile my absence. On the other, even when I leave a dominant culture, I'm still me. External noise may subside, but there is still the din of self. The imposition of rules and regulations and even removal are no substitute for the work of God. Like David, we need to cry out, "Create in me a clean heart, O God, and renew a steadfast spirit within me" (Ps. 51:10). Such prayer opens the way to re-membering as we consider again the people God has called us to join.

The spread table depicting God's grace sparks this prayer, because on this table we see evidence of God's activity. Exposed to that, we can run and hide, or we can crave the purity we encounter there. The table is set to appease our hunger; our first appetite should be for holiness. Our mouth can engage once our heart is right.

> Most merciful God,
> we confess that we have sinned against Thee
> in thought and word and deed,
> by what we have done,
> and by what we have left undone.
> We have not loved Thee with our whole heart,
> we have not loved our neighbors as ourselves . . .[3]

It is the bent of fallen hearts to move far from and to forget about God. It is the glory of God to come seeking such far-flung fruit and gather it back to himself. That image isn't completely accurate, of course—for we are not often inert citrus docile in a basket. Instead we are more like caged birds, banging against the bars, trying to make good our escape. We are, so much of the time, prone to wander.

The Spirit resident within the people of God draws us back to him, or keeps us from straying too far. Still, we jump the fences or gaze longingly into other fields. So we must examine our hearts and see what lies there. We must expose them before the Lord and say, "Remove this, and this, and this."

That will not happen easily. We will face distraction, we will rationalize, we will justify. We will object, protest, and defend. We will ignore. When we come in gathered worship to commune, we will welcome the child's tug at our sleeve, we will notice a fashion travesty, we will recall an urgent item of unfinished business. We will stop too soon or be stopped too soon. We will weep at the work of this probing.

In remembering the Lord, we are also enjoined by Paul to "recognize the body of Christ" (1 Cor. 11:29) in two ways: First, as it is presented to us through the congregation assembled. Can we see Jesus in this group, or are we inclined to notice those who offend us, who annoy us, whose very existence or peculiar habits bother us mightily? When such feelings creep into our hearts or linger there, it is time to confess our own willingness to dismantle the community. Second, we are to see Jesus in the communion, to observe that Jesus is there any time people gather in his name. Are we prepared to commune with him? Judas could not; he left before the meal was done. And us? Have our thoughts or actions betrayed him lately?

We have not loved Thee with our whole heart;
we have not loved our neighbors as ourselves.
We are truly sorry and we humbly repent.
For the sake of Thy Son Jesus Christ,
have mercy on us and forgive us;
that we may delight in Thy will,
and walk in Thy ways,
to the glory of Thy Name.
Amen.[4]

When we admit our failures, we are ready for the absolution grace offers. It releases us from the awful burden of guilt and clears the obstructions to communion and community.[5] By remembering the Lord, we come honestly and often to the One who wants us. We push aside distractions, we recall with a fresh rush of joy how much we like being in his presence, how rich our lives are because of him. Remarkably, we are quick to forget this, so we must learn to welcome our time at the table where we are reminded by simple things to fix our hearts and minds on Jesus.

"He has caused his wonders to be remembered; the LORD is gracious and compassionate" (Ps. 111:4). In communion we come to the God who prizes community, to the One who will not forget. "See," he says, "I have engraved you on the palms of my hands" (Isa. 49:16). He holds in himself mementos of us, steady reminders of his love and our need. These are the hands Jesus held out to Thomas who needed reassurance, the hands that broke and passed bread among small-minded, tough-hearted disciples. These are the hands he holds out still, saying, "Look, you're *here*." We look, and in seeing, taking, touching, tasting, we remember.

Seven

Whenever You Eat and Drink

As I write this, our youngest daughter is busy rehearsing for a school play. She files into the cafetorium with other students several times each week and even on the weekend to sing, speak, and block out scenes. Those directing these students start with warm-up exercises that sound peculiar to us as we listen to the day's tales at the dinner table; these directors send their charges home with reams of material to memorize and scrutinize. They follow a detailed schedule listing each day's actors and scenes. Reading the schedule, one sees the entire play slowly unfold and how all this labor is aimed at dress rehearsals and then performances.

I'm struck by the repetition. "Why all this time?" I wonder as I'm driving back and forth from rehearsals. "Why repeat the scenes so often?" I approach this from a novice's perspective; in high school the nearest I came to a play was operating a spotlight for one evening. My wife, more experienced, smiles knowingly, recalling her own parts in school productions. For her, the time invested is well spent.

Could these students perform after a single rehearsal, or even occasional practice? Yes. But the quality of that performance would be minimal. Its impact on both audience and players would be negligible. The rehearsals—the repetition—is necessary not simply to ensure a really big show, but to transform students into players and to transport an audience to another world.

"Do this," Jesus said as he took and passed bread (Luke 22:19), presumably directing disciples to include this meal in their routine. Paul, writing to churches about worship practices in general and the Lord's Supper in particular, includes another word from Jesus—"whenever" (1 Cor. 11:25)—for additional force.[1] Clearly Paul expected that the passing of bread and wine would be a consistent part of disciples' gatherings, but in an effort to continue the practice, concerns surface. How should communion fit into services that are often packed full with music, announcements, reports, collections, a sermon, and the like? What happens if there are "visitors" in the service? And won't frequency dilute the significance of communion?

Start with the matter of available time. Given the standard 60 to 90 minutes into which a service must fit, the worship leader frets. Facilities are often maxed out, staff is pressed, and young children past their tolerance point are not pretty. What shall we forgo in order to add communion? Consider a twin-pronged approach. Begin by examining the word *service:* Just who is being served when the congregation gathers? Who sits or stands in that "target audience"? By all means those who come deserve consideration and respect—but there is a deeper matter here. Why have they come? At whose behest? For what purpose?

After noodling over this matter, try approaching the congregation, or some manageable subset thereof. Imagine making this plea: "Communion takes time, and we can take that time from the sermon, the songs, the prayers, the conversation before, during, or after the service, testimonies, quiet reflection, the reading of Scripture. Or we can give that time from our own schedules: time from the beach, the game, homework, sleep. We can delay the preparation and consumption of food. We can be late to the sidewalk sale or grandmother's house." How might people respond? It may be that those responsible for crafting the "service" have developed, for various reasons, sensitivities that are misleading or simply wrong. It may be that with some creativity, ways around the supposed limitations can be found such that many come, or gradually learn to come, prepared to render the sacrifice that is integral to personal and corporate worship.

Next is the matter of who hears and might respond to the invitation to participate in the communion. There are "seekers" here, some will notice, people unfamiliar with the rites of the church. Curiously, very different conclusions flow from that observation. On the one hand are those who say, "Let's not confuse them or make them uncomfortable with a practice that is so obviously 'religious.'" On the other are those who warn off the uncommitted by "gating the table" and restricting it to only those properly cleared. What both groups tend to miss is the way communion can speak so eloquently about the very One such a "seeker" has been encouraged to seek.[2] By centering the table in the service it becomes

97

possible to call the attention of all present to the gospel. With the bread and cup in full view of all, the story can be told afresh, and all can be brought to the point of meaningful personal reflection.[3]

Finally, it is frequently and unequivocally said that repeated celebration will in some fashion "cheapen" communion. While granting that anything responsible for undercutting the value of a practice esteemed by the Lord and his church is to be shunned, I would still submit that this objection lacks force among those determined to prize the Supper. There is simply too much going on here to permit boredom. True, a plate and chalice, or stacks of covered trays, can be taken in with a single glance. But move a little closer; lean in and focus, and notice a tableau intricate with detail. What happens here is what we notice in a tidal pool, or under a night sky, or even in an art gallery. Stand before, say, *A Sunday Afternoon on the Island of La Grande Jatte*, the masterpiece by Georges Seurat on display at the Art Institute of Chicago. You meander into the French Impressionists section and notice this big canvas; you're attracted by the familiar, colorful scene of a crowd at the beach. Now pause. When you lean in to look more closely, you notice that this single painting is actually the result of innumerable touches of the artist's brush; each figure is a compilation of colored dots. This painting, a stunning example of Seurat's revolutionary pointillism, is textured, layered, intricate, and complex.

Some worry that frequent celebration of communion will make it ordinary. "Won't it get boring?" they ask. The concern ostensibly protects the pristine nature of communion, as though it were fresh powder that once skied is no longer quite as good. The question rises in cultures that demand variety and novelty, where repetition is as bad as stasis. We live with an amusement park mentality, where people scurry to cram all that is possible into the time that is available. Instead, we need to cultivate a "gallery" worldview. Galleries are notable for good lights and comfortable seats. Companions, stirred by their surroundings, talk quietly and well; connoisseurs shift from the printed guide to the mounted piece; students, brush in hand before their easels, spend hours or days copying a masterwork. The amusement park promotes movement, while the gallery invites inspection. One enters the park flushed and leaves exhausted. One comes to the gallery expectant and departs refreshed.

The simple fact is that Scripture does not specify the "right" frequency for celebrating communion. Even when we pull back to take in the larger picture of biblical worship, we're impressed by how few lists it includes. The themes are clear: Leviticus and Numbers stress sacrifice that revolved around the tabernacle and then the Temple, with its demands for daily, annual, and occasional offerings. Psalms insists that God be integrated into every corner of life; the prophets decry robotic ritual. In the New Testament we hear of believers gathered "on the Lord's day" but, maddeningly, we do not find a precise "order of service." Worship seems to have been less structured and more broadly conceived. It happened through care of the needy, during corporate prayer and instruction, by means of shared meals. On such occasions recollections of and reflections on God's grace and power were inevitable. In Acts' opening chapters, for example, the faith community Luke depicts crackles with vitality; there is no trace of boredom in this early church. The Spirit has struck sparks off flinty hearts that yield inextinguishable flames in people preoccupied with the Lord. His love motivates them, his power strengthens them. Others notice God in them; even enemies conclude that the reason for their behavior is exposure to Jesus.[4]

"Do this," Jesus intones, expecting that his followers will return to the simple meal where they can ponder, meditate on, choose, delight in the Lord. When? Whenever bread and cup come out among worshiping Christians. Hearts tuned to God's grace will develop rhythms and routines that honor him.

In college, a professor encouraged me to jog. I tried it because of his recommendation and a roommate's steady encouragement, and before long, I found myself a runner. The first weeks were difficult, but once the rhythm was established, I rarely missed a scheduled jog. I kept that pace until my joints protested too much, and then I exchanged running for other exercise. I had come to understand the value of building this routine into my life; it would not easily leave.

Routine can become boring, a legalistic substitute for the spontaneity of grace. But this is caused not by the thing we repeat—the meals we eat, the relationships we're part of, the job we do—as much as by the attitude we bring. It can also be the result of other decisions: We can choose to become so busy that we forgo rest and then view most everything through the haze of fatigue, or we can refuse healthy variety and calcify. We can, lacking care, fall in a rut. But if our senses stay sharp, if our hearts remain soft, if joy can bubble into laughter and pessimism or cynicism can't find a welcome, if we meet the day with grace and wonder, then even routine will be a blessing.

God built routine into us with his gift of Sabbath—a day or year in seven for re-creation and restoration. Sabbath teaches rhythm, reels in lives spun far out, counters the frantic motion so common with the true need for rest. Communion is meant to be part of that routine, another still point in a turning world, a sacred time set apart for souls pushed and pulled by idols. Communion draws us back toward what is true after we are so steadily confronted and enticed by what is merely tangible or craved. We need the routine to fend off our natural bent toward decay. This is surely part of Paul's motive when he talks about idolatry just before launching into his treatment of communion—the Corinthians were, left to their own devices, inclined to repeat the mistakes of their ancestors in the desert, who took up with pagan deities.

Idols abound; this was Moses' early cry of warning to his charges in the desert. "You will stray," he said repeatedly. "You will prefer the made over the Maker. Beware!" His warnings might fall on our carpeted floors with little effect, since today few homes sport idols of stone, wood, or precious metals on their hearths or mantels.[5] But we do well to listen, since many hearts still house alternatives to God.

A fellow came up to me after a service one evening, beaming. That was so good, he enthused. And then he proceeded to share with me a quote he'd memorized from one of the popular contemporary writers on "spirituality." I heard little of it, stunned by how little of what we had done moments ago had sunk into this guy's heart. "Each day I bless myself, looking in the mirror, seeing the god in me," he concluded. I fumbled for appropriate words.

Far too many of us have room inside for cheap imitations, and our ardor is rarely directed at the Lord.

In communion we get our bearings for managing life. We come to the table like ancient mariners with their astrolabes and staffs, who squinted at the sun several times a day in order to determine where they were and where they were going. Good navigators could tell a lot from these frequent sightings; one knew such sailors because they were often blind in one eye from looking so frequently at the sun. Routine is necessary, helpful, worthwhile—and after a while it marks you, too.

Routine requires discipline, the decision to start and stay, to weather the rough water and to paddle about in a quiet cove. Discipline is only simple sometimes; generally it demands work. But then few activities that yield good results come easy. Intriguingly, if I commit myself to an action and maintain the discipline to continue, I discover that I come to enjoy that activity, even though early on it may have been a grind. This is a difference between disciplined routine and the inevitable rut: ruts have high walls and crummy views, while routines put us on paths that afford wonderful vistas. There is also, of course, the possibility of a more random life. That appeals to some, especially those who prefer to assume little responsibility. But the supposed liberty of this approach typically ends in confusion or worse.[6]

Writer Kathleen Norris spent several years in the company of various Benedictine monks and was impressed by the routine of their lives. She observed the discipline required for such routine and points out its benefits.[7] Among these is re-formation of the person, because through discipline one's character, attitudes, and behaviors can be scrutinized and modified. The Spirit joins us in this ongoing conversion, encouraging a straightening of crooked ideals and inclinations, a focusing on what is good and true, a commitment to unnatural life, and a stand against the entropy that pulls us toward disorder and chaos. Partnering together, we engage in the discipline that pushes water uphill when human nature would rather go with the flow.

Any discipline or practice demands energy. Consider law or medicine: Those serious about their practice will study, apply themselves, and be open to new insights and conversant with what has come before. They will not fall into ruts or operate by rote but will keep searching out new facets and insisting on a fresh perspective. They will pour themselves into their discipline with verve; they will devote time to their practice, too.

We give time to what matters. It might be eradicating a slice on the fairway, or building houses for refugees, or massaging a deal near completion, but we will spend time as we see fit. Requests or demands for our time are evaluated on the basis of our own concerns: Will this interest or help me? Will non-compliance threaten me? Will this necessitate a change?

The choices we make with the time we have reflect our values. When it comes to worship, time is a concern. Preachers and service planners know this; they see the turning wrists in the congregation, hear various chimes and beeps as the hour strikes. "How do we optimize?" they ask. "How do we manage all we need to do in the allotted time? How do we slow the clock to ponder the cross, examine hearts, reflect on grace?" We deeply need release from this mentality, need to move from timetables to rhythm.

God's creation pulses with rhythm: orbits, tides, growing cycles. In worship, we can recover this fundamental pattern. Human ingenuity has interrupted natural rhythms: Light bulbs mean we can work as long as there is available power; refrigeration means we can safely store food to consume when we please; DVDs mean we can have entertainment on demand. With inventions like these, rhythms can be adjusted to suit particular purposes, and vital parts of life can be shifted or even ignored. Technology also makes us crave efficiency. I attended a seminar on service planning once and heard from the speaker that he had designated people in his congregation who timed each element of the service to track potential waste. We're responsible for more than a thousand hours each week, he told us (it was a big congregation), so we want to make sure we use them well.

Hmmm. Perhaps we would do people a service by banning timepieces from worship altogether. As we come to worship after days of tightly packed schedules, might it be good to relax and ease into a larger rhythm? Certainly there are occasions when watching the clock is productive; there are special times that bear noting. But, just as surely, there is value in easing off the fast track to listen, ruminate, and be still.

In one congregation I served, we were trying to learn this lesson. We were a group of busy people—minding families, corporations, government posts, homework—and as such we were accustomed to hurtling through our days. The frantic pace of that life entered the sanctuary if we were not careful, so we consciously took a breath as we sat. We paused to recalibrate our pace and to open our hearts. It was by assuming this vulnerable position that we were likely to be fed in body and soul. Intriguingly, when we were vulnerable enough to receive Jesus' words, we discovered the renewal and strength we suddenly realized we needed (see Ps. 119:25, 28).

The Word capable of creating still creates, and we were its beneficiaries. So we built seasons of stillness into our gathered worship. It was remarkable: we liked this. Even babies stopped their burbling as together we grew quiet. We looked forward to these moments and brought them to a close reluctantly. They became a vital part of our time together. Our congregation was not unique in this; many are discovering the value of prolonged silence. Drawing from ancient sources and newer approaches, people of faith are recovering a sense of rhythm for worship.

The church calendar helps. Its high points—Christmas and Easter—are well known, of course, but the long section between the celebration of Jesus' resurrection and First Advent bears noting, too. This is called Ordinary Time, the weeks of more regular events. Yes, Ordinary Time includes Pentecost and All Saints, occasions for more hoopla, but there is a more pervasive regularity to these months and plenty of opportunity to catch one's breath and live with an established routine.

When a meeting for corporate worship becomes an excuse for production and when the clock is ticking against all that clamors for inclusion, we have lost a sense of Ordinary Time that invites us to rest, spend time luxuriously, meander. Annie Dillard writes about Pierre Teilhard de Chardin, a Jesuit priest and renowned paleontologist. During the 1920s and 1930s, Teilhard ambled through much of China, one of the first Western scientists to probe this particular territory. His discoveries still stand as significant; his leisurely pace permitted careful attention to detail.[8] Our own pursuits may be slightly more conventional, but if I'm on a date with my new best friend and keep checking my watch, that person's going to wonder where my heart is. If I rush through a meal that's been carefully prepared and laid on the table before me, I will miss so much.[9] Same with God: if I'm so fixed on the clock that I cannot focus on him, then who is my Lord? We discover much when we slow our pace and recover a more stately rhythm.

Advent celebrates the entrance of light and life to a dead, dark world. Easter recalls how the grace of God paid to re-create what had so badly decayed, how the power of God was sufficient to beat back death and restore life. And after Easter? Life goes on, purposeful now, intentional, but absent the rush of self-created urgency. We can live, in the light of Easter, to the glory of God. Or we can squander the days in pursuit of pleasure. How we occupy ordinary time is what marks this life, the choices we make, and the values we'll cultivate that fashion the convictions we'll live by.

The practice of communion develops during ordinary time as we fall into an ancient groove to reflect on God's awesome grace and beauty. We come not because we must but because we can and because we have been invited. We gather like surfers at the end of the day to watch another radiant sunset. These have been happening regularly for a long time, but each evening brings a renewed wonder, so we wander onto the wide beach, quietly reverent before a common, startling event. Here clocks have little value; what we want more than time is space to explore, question, wonder, find. Paul's "whenever" is gloriously liberating. How often should we have communion? It's really not the right question.

Eight
You Proclaim
the Lord's Death

The frequency and style with which we celebrate communion is a matter of corporate conscience and custom, and so we should expect variety. There is meant to be, however, more uniformity with respect to its purpose. As Paul says, those who gather to break bread in memory of Jesus "proclaim the Lord's death" (1 Cor. 11:26). Coupled with Jesus' command to remember, this purpose statement can keep us from slipping into numb ritual by eliciting an awareness and proclamation of deep matters each time we are taken by the Eucharist.

Christianity insists on proclamation. Other world religions emphasize personal attentiveness, or promise solace in the face of life's inevitabilities, or simply encourage a broad and deep tolerance for animate and inanimate objects. Christianity wants to tell. There is news at the heart of this faith, a "gospel" that needs to be shared.

The Church's effectiveness in proclamation has been uneven. On the one hand, our history includes the powerful missionary movements of England and North America; more recent efforts originating in South America and Micronesia keep that torch burning. On the other, this urge to proclaim has sparked shameful episodes, battered and marginalized people, justified programs that purport to be "the" way to share the Way, and elevated practitioners to pedestals that few others can hope to occupy. Furthermore, too many studies indicate that efforts in "evangelism" do not routinely yield genuine, sustained conversion.

Where do the problems with proclamation lie? Not with the simple act of making noise—that comes easily. We wear clothing emblazoned with corporate labels, drive cars with prominent logos, and eat food wrapped in distinctive packaging. We cultivate and trumpet tastes and preferences; we have ready answers for what we'd like for our birthdays or Christmas. We pierce, brand, and tattoo statements in our flesh. Enormous scoreboards at athletic stadiums bear messages of love and invitations to marriage; cloth banners hung from college dormitories or dining halls do the same thing. No, proclamation is rarely a challenge.

Our trouble starts with the matter of content.[1] We face sizable obstacles here because what we are to proclaim is a potent, messy cross. It is easier, safer, to talk instead about other entry points to the life of Christian faith; so we dwell, for instance, on how a relationship with God will help people. Too rarely do we admit that it means to kill them first. That seems an overly harsh message and unlikely to attract others.

We hesitate, or we go partway by glossing the cross, displaying it polished and smooth in ears, on lapels, across bumpers. Sometimes in painting and sculpture artists dare to wrestle with the vividness of crucifixion, but often such art, in church buildings or museums, is surrounded by stained glass or pastoral landscapes which swathe its rough edges in bubble wrap. A carpenter friend emerged from his basement one evening with a cross he had built for a church display. He was a strong guy but bowed beneath the weight of this ungainly weathered timber. Gingerly setting it on the floor and leaning it against a wall, he whispered, "It sort of takes your breath away." It did, and it does. This cross towers above all else; it explains and indicts much of what passes for evangelism among us.

During my first year of college I worked briefly with an organization that focused on discipling high school students. An older fellow mentored me in the ways of this group as we talked about strategy and results. Key to success in his mind was our ability to find the winners, the really popular kids at school, and help them become peer leaders. When we go after that kind of person, he would tell me, others will follow.

One evening in the car on the way back to my dorm, talk turned to theology. I forget what got us started, but eventually we came to the root message of Christianity. "I preach Christ crucified," I said, quoting Paul like any eager freshman. The other fellow paused. "No," he responded, "we preach Christ resurrected."

"That's not the way Paul put it," I said. "He said, crucified." The other fellow stood firm: "Resurrected. It's a positive message," he told me. "Positive."

Not long after, we parted ways. I have often thought about that exchange; it drove me more than once to read Paul's statement (1 Cor. 1:23) and its context. And I think I finally hit upon the problem my erstwhile boss had encountered: a crucified Christ seems somehow incomplete. Almost a loser.

No good Christian denies the crucifixion, but few of us want to linger there. We're perfectly willing to acknowledge Good Friday, of course, but we'd rather be plowing into Easter with all the verve of a rugby scrum. This is where the action is! Crucifixion, we muse, is more preamble.

Paul would disagree strongly. He begins his letter to Corinth on the note of crucifixion since apparently the followers of Jesus there had begun to question the centrality of the cross or its role in their daily lives. "Is this to be our symbol?" they wondered. "The banner around which we rally?" "Yes," states the apostle emphatically. He doesn't drift far from the point, either, reminding them throughout the epistle of how their own petty concerns often failed to reckon with the heart of the gospel, where the good news of grace counters the bad news of what sin has brought about. Christians are people who admit to personal sin, recognize its damning effect, and cry out for help. They discover on the cross One who died in their place, assuming the penalty they deserved. They ponder this gracious mercy often; communion helps.[2] Consideration of the death of Jesus prepares one for following his example: Disciples also commit themselves to death. Paul's explanation, that those taking communion "proclaim the Lord's death" (1 Cor. 11:26), covers the waterfront. "You are harbingers of death," Paul affirms. "Of the Lord's, and then your own, and then the death of others."

Death is a hard sell. Much of our life goes into the business of living. Ask people why they fear going to the doctor, or why they are repulsed by disease, or why the threat of cancer produces such emotion, and they will say, if honest, "I do not care to die." It is not my time, we think; we are too young, or too busy, or not sufficiently prepared. Our oldest daughter finished high school in a trice and then left for college one day. The night before, I sat on the edge of the bed, overwhelmed. "I knew this day was inevitable," I told my wife. "But did it have to come so soon?" This is how we feel about death, too: we know it to be certain, but it seems so often to take us by surprise.

Not only that, but we resist death with all the energy we can muster. We cling to life more than a limpet holds to coral; we will not go quietly into the night. So we jog, medicate, and watch our intake of fat and sodium. We pound into life like hail, except that we are determined to last. Some slip in their resolve: "He's lost his will to live," the doctors say of the patient who fades away. Others nod, educated by film and TV: "If only he'd been more willing to live," they think, "everything would have come out right."

We rarely speak of the will to die. This is one reason Jesus routinely baffles—he talks so much about death. That's uncomfortable, and so we gravitate to something more practical, more homey. Another parable, maybe, or an anecdote—those would be better than more of that depressing obsessing on death. But this misses what is virtually the first thing out of Jesus' mouth when he goes public. "Come, follow me," Jesus says (Mark 1:17). And

111

just where is he going? And perhaps more to the point, through what does he go? Same answer both times: to die, through death. He "resolutely set out" toward Jerusalem (Luke 9:51), where he would die; from this course of action he could not be dissuaded. This hardly seems like a victory march.

We, on the contrary, avoid death at every opportunity and shudder when it comes near. When the passing truck swerves and narrowly misses our own vehicle, we notice our pulse pounding, our breath rapid. Why? "He almost nailed me," we say. *I nearly died,* we think. *Whew.* When one reports that another has cancer, we are curious; we want to know more. We wonder whether the lump on our shoulder or the blotch on our skin could be cancer, too. Might we also, like this poor soul whose story alternately both repels and attracts us, be on the fast track to death? Hope not. Death bothers, annoys, scares us. It's unwelcome and inconvenient. It disrupts plans and relationships. It rarely comes at the right time. As we used to say in college, "Sure, I'm ready to die—after I get married."

People of faith wrestle with death. Our books are full of brave tales, and we often believe these, but when death comes close, we're not as certain. Does death hold a surprise—something the books don't, or can't, anticipate? We wonder.

Stories of "near-death experiences" vaulted to popularity for a time. In such volumes came tales of accidents, diseases, crashes, or fadings that led to the brink of death when suddenly there was a leap back into the land of the living. People who should have died saw lights, heard voices, discerned blurred figures; they reported messages, they came away relieved. Books like these were bought in case lots and passed around eagerly. But they promised more hope than they could deliver.

Near death. We are all near death each day.

The first funeral I performed as a young pastor was for a family in our church. Both parents had come to faith at our kitchen table; each had been growing in the faith and in our church. She carried a baby for a while and then gave birth to a boy who lived for a dozen hours. "Do you want to hold him?" the anguished father asked as I walked into the hospital room where they stood shortly after the delivery. What do you say to this when the infant before you is so small, so twisted, so impossible? You think of your own kids, hale and hearty; you think of this one's sibling, a budding athlete. You look into the face of death and see an eye twitch. The emotions overwhelm. The loss bites into your heart, aching like the phantom limb that recent amputees describe. You are sure what is missing is there; you can feel it. But one look confirms: She isn't coming home; that baby is still dead. And your heart has a leak too large to plug.

We buried this child a short time later; we ate pie in the grandparents' living room afterwards. Death is no easy companion. This is why, I expect, we seek company after funerals. We sit with others and fork into ourselves reminders that we are not the interred; there is still some meat on these bones, still some breath in these lungs. Another piece of chicken? That bread sure smells good.

There is, even among people of faith, a tentativeness about death that only exacerbates the problem. Thankfully, there are also among us those who face death squarely and help us face it too. The pastor of a congregation in California learned he had inoperable cancer and announced this discovery one Sunday. "As a pastor, I came," he said, "with what I thought was a mandate from God to preach the gospel and to challenge each of you about living for him. It would seem now that as your pastor it will be my challenge to teach you how to die." A year later he was gone, but the lesson had sunk in.

Another family steeped in faith maintained a bedside vigil after a supposedly routine surgery left their daughter inexplicably comatose. One or another of the parents would send mail like this to supporters:

It's been an incredible journey thus far. And we may not even yet be to the middle.

A few days ago when I picked up Gail's beautiful little hand to exercise her fingers, I had visions of being in a hospital in Lima, Peru, forty-two years ago when I first picked up that same beautiful little hand. All the fingers were there and so perfect. At that time I thought ahead to all that those hands would be capable of doing. And she has done so much more than just fulfill that new mother's thoughts. So to sit by Gail's bedside today and watch her needing to depend on something other than herself to even breathe at times breaks my heart. I love her so much.

For the first few weeks of this experience, I told myself that this just couldn't be happening. It's just too unreal. After that came the phase of accepting that it really is happening, but wondering how we deal with it. (Could I say with Joseph of Genesis that "God means it for good"?) Then it was that we saw how to deal with it—but what about Gail's future?

At the same time my prayer focus has been going through similar changes. When I first stood by Gail's bed and pleaded "Lord God, heal her," I was almost immediately struck by the thought that here I was, a human voice, telling the Creator of the universe what to do. What audacity! Then the words, "But Lord, you know my heart" came to quell my fears and bring peace. By immersing myself in the Word over the next days, I continued to pray for Gail's healing and be thankful that all of you were also interceding on her behalf.

The more I read, the more the passages about "giving thanks in ALL things" came to my attention. Really, in all things, Lord? Of course, I've been down this road before, but I may just be a slow learner. So about the same time I accepted Gail's helpless condition, I began to shift my prayers from petition to praise. To thank God that our daughter may be dying or may be in this helpless state for a long, long time is a giant step of faith. Nevertheless, in obedience and by faith, God gave me the willingness to do just this.[3]

Moses sets this example for us, too, asking that God would "teach us to number our days aright" (Ps. 90:12). This "prayer of the man of God"[4] is full of reference to and awareness of death, but absent of any morbid fascination with dying. Moses seems intent on making life count, on having it fit into the steady flow of past generations and influence those yet to come. Death is part of life, neither to be stalked nor shunned. Once we reckon with death, we can get on with life, operating with hearts of wisdom and being glad all our days (Ps. 90:12, 14).

A pastor friend uses a borrowed line in his funeral oratories: "It may be too late for _____, but what about you?" He wants his listeners to consider their prospects, wants that casket to send a message. So does Paul. You proclaim the Lord's death, he says. When you tear that loaf, sip from that cup, you are touching something tangible. Are you awake enough to sense that? Will you

115

permit death to steal into your heart this day and force you to reckon with your own mortality? More importantly, will you, as a follower of Jesus, lay down your life with him? Because let's face it: he wants you to die.

Early Christians were condemned as cannibals because popular misconceptions about communion had them feasting on human flesh. It surprises me that they weren't more often branded as murderers, with all their talk about the need to die. Within the ranks, language eventually morphed, and the interest in death became a fascination with martyrdom. Dying for the cause was elevated precipitously; people clamored for the honor. Many died this way with sincere hearts; some probably got swept up by the sheer romanticism of it. Strange, that death would actually be welcomed, but read some of these early accounts and you see that there's little more than that in play at times.

An overemphasis on martyrdom misses Jesus and Paul. Certainly a commitment to follow Jesus unto death, however literally, is commendable in some settings, but just what does the Lord want? In some cases surely he is honored by the martyr. In others—in most?—it is something more mundane: he wants a death that can be followed by resurrection in this world.

Death, like a shadow, is not always seen, but never far away. We cannot out of fear or denial avoid death. We need not embrace it to the point of morbid fascination, either, but do well to cultivate an accurate view. When we acknowledge the reality of death, we will be able to receive every waking moment as more miraculous than guaranteed. We will also be prepared both to live and to die "unto the Lord" (Rom. 14:8 KJV).[5]

The Lord bids all his followers to come and die[6] so that they can have a hope for life. If we skip the dying part, then the living isn't worth all that much. What does it profit one to gain the world but lose the soul? And the soul, he tells us, is recoverable only after the severe trauma of death. It is precisely this trauma, however, that we'd like to avoid; we'd rather give death a pass. We seek a simpler way, less messy, less demanding. Death, after all, is so final. But die we must, because he did. And in dying he sets a pattern we are to notice and herald.

For a long time I read Paul's statement in 1 Corinthians 11:26 as though it were incomplete. In my mind, and occasionally in public when I had opportunity, I would help Paul finish his thought: "You proclaim the Lord's death . . . *and resurrection,*" I would add, certain Paul would have agreed. What I finally see, though, is his commitment to the cross. I shouldn't have been so slow to this, so hesitant to embrace the death of Jesus. When I am able to read the phrase as it is written, a diamond emerges, both hard and brilliant, glimmering in the meal that brings us to Calvary.

We should be aware of communion's purpose as we approach the table, but often we miss its point about Jesus' death and that the Lord who calls people to himself wants the same for them. We can, for instance, get caught up in the mechanics and choreography of serving the elements to a large crowd. We can rush through it, tacking communion on to a service for the sake of tradition. We can fixate on one aspect of the ritual, perhaps becoming only and always somber. We can make it so mysterious as to be inaccessible.

117

Communion encourages us to remember; it exhorts us to proclaim. We are neither passive consumers of what appears before us nor paying customers expecting to have our senses sated. We come to be confronted, changed, taken. We affirm in communion that the death of Jesus is essential, and we declare our desire for "becoming like him in his death" (Phil. 3:10).[7] By proclaiming the Lord's death, we announce agreement with necessary change. My life, we say, is of little consequence; I give it gladly and freely to the Lord. In the transaction of faith, we sign the waiver releasing our hold on life. It now belongs to God, to do with as he will.

We find reluctance in some quarters: too many family farms have been sold to shopping mall magnates and leveled in favor of pavement. Will the same happen here? Will all we've worked for, all we've accumulated get plowed under and forgotten once we've signed on with God? A rich young man Jesus met had that concern. "Sell all you have if you want to join me," the Lord directed. The fellow walked away sad "because he had great wealth" (Mark 10:22). His holdings defined him, held him, and he clung passionately to them, unable to let go, unwilling to die.

At the table we make a declaration of dependence to the Lord, to ourselves, and to the gathered company of believers and seekers[8] as we lay down the arms with which we would otherwise defend our esteemed selves. We give over our supposed rights to life and liberty, releasing them into the hands of the Lord, who can then do as he pleases. And as is often the case, he returns life to us to be lived for his glory. For God is not one who simply wants to *take*. His program is to exchange the way we are inclined to live with another that will be of

118

greater benefit. When people yield to him, they make space he can fill. Full of grace, God gives.

Manifestations of this grace come to us as we recline at the table: We become aware of how richly blessed our life is once it has passed through the gateway of Jesus' cross. We discern the rich spiritual blessings of inclusion in God's family, the sure reality of his Spirit's presence. We find in this time at table that our hearts are full of gratitude and that in gratitude we are all the more inclined and eager to serve. Situations and people come to mind, and we discover that there is in us both a desire to help and the resources for doing so. What begins as a hand on the knob of death's door concludes with a quickened step in the life God marks out. Progress is possible and certain, grounded in the reality of what Jesus has done.[9]

While helping with a service in a Florida funeral home, I overheard two older ladies discussing the recent deaths of other friends. Their conversation was casual, as routine as neighbors discussing crabgrass. Listening, I understood why: these two had seen a lot of death in their day. For them an afternoon spent at the funeral parlor was becoming common. The mystique was evaporating, and they could accept death as part of life.

Communion desensitizes our aversion to death. When the rough texture of bread scratches our fingers and scrapes our tongue; when the rush of cool liquid softens our throat and hurtles south, we are forced to sense these elemental reminders of mortality. And with the body energized by sustenance, with the voice lubricated by this wee dram, we can proclaim his death.

119

Nine

Until He Comes

Jesus is coming again

How do you punctuate this sentence? For many raised in the church, a simple period will do. We acknowledge that Jesus will return; that is a fixed point on the list of propositions in our doctrinal statement. I wonder, though, whether Paul, or John, or Peter, or Priscilla would have been happy with a period. I suspect that each of them, and many more who lived close to the Lord, would have insisted on an exclamation point or three.

Jesus is coming again!

Oceans of doctrinal ink awash on acres of theological pages sometimes numb us to the simple, apathy-shattering idea that Jesus is on his way back for his own. This dense, glimmering truth is meant to draw us through difficult days and knotty relationships and snippy meetings and meager larders—not because it casually dismisses the reality around us but because it emphasizes what is so much more real.

We fill the future with dreams or fears; we anticipate reward or dread recompense. The writer of Hebrews has a different perspective, speaking of it in terms of hope that anchors a soul (6:19). Hope? This is the Bible's word for what lies out at the horizon, certain as the setting sun; hope by such a definition tosses us into the future. Anchor? We might think to throw an anchor into the already known past, or at the least into the tangible present. But citizens of Christ's kingdom do neither. They set their stake in the future. Hear Paul, who picks up on Jesus' words: "Whenever you eat and drink," he said, referring to the bread and cup of communion, "you proclaim the Lord's death *until he comes*" (see 1 Cor. 11:26). Paul's reference to the soon coming of Jesus slams the oven door on the soufflé of puffy notions about time. The future is not smoke but a mirror which reveals something about our hearts. The future is steady, solid, dependable—sufficient for building and sustaining a life *now*.

Jesus spoke often about what was still ahead; in this he was like the prophets. Those seers delivered their messages not to amaze people with fantastic predictions but to cultivate hope that would in turn affect behavior. Looking into the future and then speaking to those living now, these prophets addressed fundamental concerns of the kingdom—like charity, peace, faith—all of which were rooted in God who holds all in his hand. Jesus too saw this God and described him; he urged people to look for God, to count on him, to anticipate the time of union with him such that the anticipation influenced every aspect of their existence. We have made Jesus' talk of the future a matter of chronology. Jesus saw the future in terms of ethics.

Several of my family's early vacations involved camping in various parks. We would trail an ancient pop-up behind our van and once we reached our destination, open hatches, unbuckle snaps, and winch up canvas siding. For extra room we'd unpack a small tent, snap poles together, slide fabric over them, and secure the floor with plastic pins. Often the ground below was soft and sandy, due to our preference for camping near beaches. I recall more than once a stiff wind or an unwanted rain lifting that tent or ruffling our pop-up. An hour or two of that was bearable, sometimes even exciting for suburbanites accustomed to snug protection from the elements. But a full night of howling winds or rising water made some of us brittle as china.

Those tents were strikingly different from a project I worked on when my father decided to add a room off the back of our house for my brother and me. First he marked off with strings the area to be covered; then we began to dig. I recall the bite of a pick into limestone for trenches where concrete would form "footers"; we'd scrape, shovel, measure, and chop more rock. Finally cement came, filling those long, deep lines and rising to make a floor. Late that afternoon Dad came out with heavy steel stakes in his hand—anchor bolts, he called them—which he began to pound in methodically around the perimeter. The threaded end of each bolt stuck up from the concrete a full three inches, puncturing an otherwise smooth surface.

When the cement had dried and cured, we laid on lumber, starting with long pieces of treated two-by-six that would sit atop the concrete. Walls would be built on these plates, but first we drilled holes for the bolts so we could cinch the wood tight to the concrete with a washer and nut. The walls that rose were then fixed to the floor, which itself was resting on a solid foundation.

Our tents blew over in mild gusts; this new room stood firm when the tails of hurricanes whipped through our yard. The difference? Anchors. Steel and cement bonded and bolt grabbed board firmly, each clinging to the other so that walls, roof, furniture, and teenage boys would not be blown away.

Anchors have prongs that dig in and hold fast; once set, they influence what is attached at the other end. They limit movement, of course, but this is expected and intentional, as an anchor is not thrown casually. They also provide a measure of safety and stability. When people anchor themselves to the Coming One, they discover ties to the Lord which affect for good the life they lead.

The apostle John makes this point in his Revelation, an apocalyptic piece of writing often read for details in constructing an elaborate timetable. But come to Revelation with a journal to reflect on what is flowing into and out from your heart rather than with a calendar to plot dates and events. The book begins on an isolated island where John sees the glowing "son of man" (1:12–16) and concludes in a teeming city where the Lord, seated on a throne, is making all things new (21:5). We are drawn to him as we read, propelled into the future by past prophecies and events, compelled to consider the "Coming One." John paints the picture rapidly; he seems barely able to tear himself away from the vision of Jesus long enough to describe everything else adequately.

John urges us to "look," promises that "every eye will see him," and knows that "all peoples of the earth will mourn because of him" (1:7). That last phrase catches attention—why all the weeping? Several reasons, surely: Some will, at Jesus' appearing, be suddenly mindful of their willful disobedience; some will rue that life as they know it has ended; some will be torn by the knowledge that loved ones will now be separated. And some—perhaps many—will be instantly aware of how little they loved the Lord who spoke often of his certain return.

While on earth, the Lord promised that he would not only depart but also come back. We affirm that, but seem by the way we live to set less stock by it. In the rough and tumble of daily life, concerns creep in and the Lord leaks out. Steady rains find holes to fall through and make hearts sag; strong winds tear at small imperfections and make larger gashes; quakes shake hasty buildings; garbage collects; dust moose multiply; gardens go unweeded. Hell comes, or high water; sometimes we simply drift away in even gentle breezes, like dandelion pods. Like the Ephesians, we find or fall into ways that lead us to forsake our first, best love (Rev. 2:4).

So how does one stay close? It starts with hammering bolts into solid ground, and then continues by tying on to those firm holds in faith, taking hold of him who is gracious enough to reach out and connect with us. We reflect on his work on our behalf, and we anticipate the fulfillment of what this faithful God says is yet to occur. Not one of these actions is automatic, natural, or easy; not one is written on our hearts with indelible ink. To make matters worse, we are slow learners, too, and we forget so easily what once we had learned so well. And if that weren't enough, we are actively suspicious of the future, which is why we work incessantly to insulate life in the present and so often take refuge in the past.

Jesus does not ignore the past. Indeed, as he holds bread and wine before his disciples, he calls them to remember. That is a bid toward what has happened already—although at this point, the main event he has in mind is still to come. His words here prepare them for later celebrations in the kingdom after the cross slices open life as they know it. A moment later, however, he slings them much further afield. Still holding that loaf and cup, he promises that he will not again drink like this until all gather for a marvelous banquet in the fully realized kingdom of God (Mark 14:25).[1] Again, we're accustomed to reading this section, hearing it read, and winding up with a period: Take this bread, take this cup, I won't drink again until I drink anew in the kingdom. Period.

Re-punctuate. Replace the period with ellipses or an exclamation point. Link this saying with John 14:3, where Jesus promises to return and collect his own so that they can be together forever. Allow the joy of this anticipated moment to seep through and permeate the melancholy so common among those who are weighed down by the vicissitudes of life. "Until he comes" reminds disciples that the story is unfinished, that there is to come not more of the same but that which is truly wonderful. As satisfying as a traditional Passover meal was, the dinner this night, along with those that would follow, was not the *tour de force* Jesus had in mind. It's like what happens when my extended family gathers for a reunion. We come from all over as often as we can, with the latest babies in tow, to join the matriarchs and patriarchs flush with the happiness of reunion. Packed elbow to elbow around a table rich with memories, conversation roams. We're a bunch of cooks and bakers, with recipes and menus that have been around for generations, so we recall previous repasts; we talk about produce, hunting season, gardens, sales. Amid the rollicking humor of these meals there is also always a tinge of sadness because we know they will end and that we will part. So while munching on carrots, wiping a spill, or admiring a pie, we start planning; what happens here primes the pump for our next meal. Anticipation crowds sorrow as we ask and affirm: where will you be, and how can we meet, and surely soon we will gather in a wonderful place for a marvelous feast with even more people.

As eager as he was to celebrate this evening's Passover with his disciples, Jesus was looking ahead to the really big feast, to the time when he would gather his entire family without threat of disruption to enjoy a meal over which all could linger. Now, might Jesus have said such things with a gleam in his eye and a smile spreading across his face? Might his voice have risen a bit, conveying a sense of excitement and anticipation? Is it possible that he looked at these people and said, "You can expect rough roads ahead, but take heart—this won't last forever. There's more to come, and far better. Wait for it, and while you're waiting, don't forget what's still to come."

So we do: We wait. That's got its own challenges, as any kid near Christmas, any photographer lying in the savannah, any runner anticipating race day knows. Anticipation can be exciting for a while and send thrills down spines or raise lumps in throats. But after time passes, the waiting weighs us down. This is one reason why God, through his Spirit, gives patience (see Gal. 5:22–23).

Patience is the virtue given by God that makes it possible to sit easy with the wait of our worlds. Patience makes it possible to accept what comes as from God's hands and to move in ways that persistently bring honor to him. Patience helps us balance past, present, and future. Anxiety, one antithesis of patience, is the fretfulness of an unsure life: I fret when I am disrupted from my reverie, when I grow upset with what I encounter, when expectations (at least those formed within an uncounseled heart) are disappointed. Fretfulness robs us of the benefits of submitting to a schedule and to developments that are trustworthy but not of our own devising.[2]

Anxiety withers and patience flourishes as we learn to develop what Thomas Merton described as a "clear, unobstructed vision of the true state of affairs, an intuitive grasp of one's inner reality as anchored, or rather lost, in God through Christ."[3] The restlessness caused by trying to control what is frequently and ultimately beyond our grasp dissipates as we entrust our minutes, hours, and years to the Lord and rest in the faith that he is alive and engaged. It is an "active" rest, as patience is not attained by becoming inert or indifferent. It develops as we notice the work of God through Christ—the very work we celebrate at the table of communion and which becomes for people of faith a secure point for anchorage. Given the inevitable storms and our own interior fault lines, we need this meal until he comes.

From such patience, joy emerges as we recognize that our own puny efforts to control circumstances are unnecessary and that the One we trust delights in being trustworthy. In securing both past and future in the sure work of God, Paul is saying that the present too can be entrusted to the Lord. Those with faith in God can count on him for safe anchorage and so can move through their days in ways that consistently bring him honor. The cross, where the "death" we proclaim was accomplished, pushes us forward, impelling us toward the "worthy" life (Eph. 4:1).[4] We are pulled, too, toward the time and place of reunion with Christ and steadily urged to keep our eyes up and straining ahead in eager anticipation "until he comes." Such hope hammered into a heart and mind anchors the soul for any weather.

Jesus is coming again!!!

Ten

Who Is the Greatest?

Nothing quite prepares you for approaching the Grand Canyon. You're flying west from the Mississippi, skimming the barren expanse of the Arizona desert, when all of a sudden the ground opens. Even at 25,000 feet, the gap is impressive. Imagine what it was like for early explorers.

You can see those first scouts, galloping far ahead of the shambling wagon train. Suddenly a horse pulls up short, and then the rider notices the vast, jagged incision. "How do we get around this?" the guide wonders. From that day forward, every person who travels this route will know of the enormous crevice; all journeys west will have to reckon with this slash into the earth's crust.

God is like this: You make your way through life, picking out trails, dodging the occasional snake hole or mountain lion, foraging food and water off the land until one day you walk smack into him. *How* did you find him? People report a wide range of experiences, and theologians, as expected, quarrel about who found whom, but what's significant is that a meeting occurred. You will spend the rest of your life either getting closer to or further from him because God is, like the Grand Canyon, too big to avoid.

God's greatness can come as a relief for those seeking Another outside themselves who is competent, powerful, aware, interested, and committed. People like this sink thankfully into the enormity of God, glad to be awed. They are in the company of psalmists who cry, "Great is the LORD and most worthy of praise; his greatness no one can fathom" (Ps. 145:3), and "Praise him for his acts of power; praise him for his surpassing greatness" (Ps. 150:2).

For others, the magnitude of God comes as a threat, like the new kid who transfers into high school from another state—the kid who is tall, tan, smart, and rich, and who can sink the shot from half court every time—or the bright spark with impeccable credentials and a winning personality bumped up by the home office five years ahead of schedule. People like this make some cringe, make them seek a weakness, a soft spot for criticism or disdain. It's paradoxical: We fuel the competitive urge early and aggressively with advanced classes for the "gifted" and clinics, coaches, and leagues aimed at producing championship athletes, and then we criticize those who excel. It's hard for human egos the size of time zones to think another might pull out ahead. So one walks or runs, head swiveling. Who's better? Who's the best? We're dying to know and to have it proclaimed.

Among the disciples gathered for dinner with Jesus, a debate that had surfaced before popped out once again: "Among us," some ask of the Lord, "who is the greatest?"

(Luke 22:24). The question is surely rhetorical, and begs a single answer: "Me." What makes these disciples so laughable, so poignant, is the way they give voice to our own hearts' secrets. Which of us hasn't walked into a room and done a quick evaluation of the people there? We're comparing, placing, figuring ways to emerge on or at least near the top. Who is the greatest, indeed—the answer is plain, isn't it? And yet a small doubt gnaws like a mouse with cheese under the sink. I am—but all the same, I'd like to be sure. Especially since there's a group of us.

There are many around Jesus, sincere in their devotion or benign in their skepticism. Many trail along, hanging on his words, looking for a meal, hankering for a miracle or a rousing rebuke of the religious hotshots, hoping that he is the One they have been seeking. From among these, Jesus selects a smaller band and pours himself into them. We know little of the interpersonal dynamics within this collection of twelve merchants, politicians, and family men—but we know a little. We know, for instance, of their thickness concerning the nature of Jesus. We are also aware that despite Jesus' special interest, they still jockey for position. The Gospels record two occasions when the question of rank captured the disciples' attention. One is while they sit at the table with Jesus on the eve of his arrest and trial. The other came earlier, after Jesus had gone with three up a mountain and been transfigured. Interesting that in such contexts such a question is raised. Even at holy times, minds wander.

On that mountain, Jesus had shone like the sun. He had talked with Moses and Elijah, had been approved by the heavenly voice. On that mountain Peter, speaking for the other disciples who had accompanied Jesus, had offered to build shelters to commemorate the event or to symbolize the intent of a glorified God to dwell now among his people—but Peter had been silenced: "Don't do anything," boomed the thunderous voice. "Just listen." The greatness of the Lord was unmistakable on that mountain, but what the disciples experienced there quickly fled from their hearts. A few hours later they were embroiled with their other companions in a comparison of one another: "Who among us is the greatest?"

Jesus thinks this is a problem—but why? Isn't a little jostling okay? Might it not even toughen us a bit, make us better able to cope with all the shoving we're likely to encounter as we move through life? Apparently not, at least as far as Jesus is concerned. From his perspective, such questions opened doors into noxious space. Either they led people to push God off the screen in favor of their own selves, or they fostered a competition that was inherently dangerous.

Our geography teacher walked into class at the beginning of a term and surveyed the room. "There are five of you in this class," he said (it was a small school), "which means that one will receive an A, one a B, one a C, and so on" (it was also a somewhat rigorous school). We stirred uncomfortably in our seats. Each person in this room was a friend of mine; one was my own brother. Now we all faced a problem that set us at odds with each other: success would come at someone else's expense.

Community suffers from competition. When members pit themselves against others, or invite comparisons, or think themselves above certain tasks or people, trouble within the community is inevitable. Compatriots who interrupt pursuit of a common goal for criticism, bombast, or arrogance soon find that the "common life" has ground to a halt. As with all since Adam, the "son of God" fashioned from dust, the struggle is between rising towards godliness and sinking into the mud. Competition separates, isolates. It introduces to an otherwise healthy body a deadly toxicity or a harmful element that induces an allergic reaction. Appallingly, we hardly notice what is happening. Casual language, marketplace exchanges, and popular publications routinely describe the work we do, the people we encounter, the positions we stake out and defend in terms of games and battles. No wonder we move through our days fierce, stressed, and wary.

Brothers stand back to back. "Who is taller?" one asks the mother. Then, a few years later, a son stands against the back of his father. "Who is taller?" he wonders. We go through life like this, comparing ourselves to those around us. Should our worlds expand, that only increases the field of comparison.

When eventually God enters that field, we have been sufficiently trained or conditioned to view him similarly: Who is taller? Of course, some measure of reverence or respect will require us to give him the edge, but by how much? A quick examination of many lives provides the answer: not much. We find ways to tilt the book, to slope the hand, and then to say: "We're nearly the same. Right?" Do this often enough and God shrinks.

What is the effect of such language and posture on community? Competition divides people; it splits apart what might otherwise knit together. One of our daughters slipped on ice and gashed her leg. A doctor applied a butterfly bandage and three stitches, but the next day our kid went skiing. She could have stayed quiet and still, allowing the restorative impulses of her wounded leg time to bind the tissue, but she preferred motion, action. Today she sports a scar, a reminder of how easily things pull apart.

In plate tectonics, a child's skin, or interpersonal dynamics, pushing and pulling promotes rupture. Integrity is far more likely where there is quiet and stillness. People trying to restore shattered hearts and bones know this; they seek the tranquility of a beach or mountain lake rather than the jostling of a shopping mall sale. "Seek peace and pursue it," counsels David (Ps. 34:14); "in quiet and trust is your strength" (Isa. 30:15). Who is the greatest? It is a jarring interjection, sure to tear the fellowship of Jesus' company. No good can come of following this question to its end; no one "wins" with a direct answer.

Instead, Jesus changes course twice. First, he draws a child into the circle of jostling men (Matt. 18:2–4; Luke 9:47–48). "If you insist on comparing yourself to another, then choose this," he says, pointing to the young one. We think from this example that Jesus wants us to be gentle, curious, unconcerned. Maybe. And then, maybe he just wants us to be small. That grates, but it better fits his point. "You focus on achieving greatness," he says in different ways. "Why? Isn't it enough to be linked to God? Relax and develop comfort in your smallness—smallness, that is, as compared with God."[1]

Next, he commends service (Mark 9:35; Luke 22:26). He anticipates the life sure to face those intent on following him and reflects on his own experience. The goal, he suggests, is not to place yourself above others around you but rather at their disposal. For when you give yourself to the King, you have given yourself away. In the kingdom of God, you are his to do with as he pleases, and you need no longer to concern yourself with what it takes to win or to scratch the itch of pride. As a member of his company, you are finally freed from the need to compete and so able to work together toward a common end. The effort once spent on pushing ahead of others can now be directed at linking arms to accomplish what brings God glory.

We confuse getting attention with paying attention. We were created to render praise, not to receive it, and our lives should be more similar to the prophet Amos who was a watcher of sheep and a tender of trees. We must tend to godliness with the fervor of a shepherd or gardener, and this is no easy task, especially when that urge for recognition creeps in, dragging a spotlight and microphone. Amma Syncletica knew this long before the added inducements of the electronic age. This fourth-century ascetic wisely said, "It is impossible for us to be surrounded by worldly honor and at the same time to bear heavenly fruit."[2]

The "desert fathers" of early centuries realized that one of the disciple's legitimate battles lay within a single heart. This is why they regularly threw themselves into the harshest of surroundings and pulled the dark austerity of caves around them in order to wrestle with the vagaries of their own natures. Others stood back in awe or shyly came to seek assistance for similar struggles. Many, of course, ignored them altogether and simply went their own way. But for all the peculiarities of diet and dress, for all the stories of demonic encounters real and imagined, for all the paucity of creature comforts, these people exerted a profound influence on the church.

They scoured the minds of Augustine, Benedict, and many more—people whose own influence was considerable. Having learned to rein in base desires, they esteemed not dominance but self-control. They lifted the Lord high, far above their own selves; they lived to worship, eschewed comfort, preferred others over themselves. One story is given about a pair of desert monks who upon meeting each other for the first time spent a day each waiting for the other to break the bread of their meal.[3]

A question like "Who is the greatest?" erupts from a heart turned in on its own advancement and indifferent to the health of the larger body. Sometimes it is voiced directly, asked by those like these disciples eager for clarity in placement and position. Sometimes it is more covert, banging around in brains and hearts but emerging in other forms—the arrogance of self-reliance and self-aggrandizement, the depression of unrealized expectations and aspirations, the bluster from people who do not receive the recognition they believe they deserve.[4] Then insecurities swirl, accusations fly, anger erupts, defenses go up, competition emerges, pitched battles ensue—and community suffers.

Those tasked with the care of souls need to reckon with the depth of this urge to compete, to separate, to *win*. They need to recognize the forms in which this urge expresses itself and then to focus on the real issue and not the apparent problem. Occasionally this means calling to account those who, by means of loud voice and violent action, slam doors in the household of faith. As Dietrich Bonhoeffer says, "reproof is unavoidable" and "rebuke must be ventured." He writes with compassion, advocating patience, meekness, forbearance, careful listening, and humble service. But this Lutheran pastor also knows that when people gather for life together, even under the banner of Jesus, there can still be considerable friction. So for Bonhoeffer there are occasions when "we must speak the judging and dividing Word of God"[5] across the rifts that threaten community.

It takes wisdom, compassion, and discernment to do this well, because sometimes stupid questions are innocently raised, and sometimes they voice the corruption in a heart. But generally such queries have a common cause: they belie a smoldering pride. So Jesus must often patiently remind or loudly proclaim that the path to greatness means accepting smallness: "Whoever wants to become great among you must be your servant" (Matt. 20:26). He's talking about service on his terms, not ours. Our preference is to serve only as we see fit: to be kind, but only to those I like; to pitch in vigorously, but only for a while; to bear a load, but only until something more appealing comes along. We fail to notice that what we mistake for greatness is only limelight. Elusive and insubstantial, that beam eventually dims, or other, brighter lights outshine it, and our own positions are finally exposed as ephemeral. Jesus advocates service for God's sake and according to his way.

In the end, an insistence on being great is another way of revoking the authority of Jesus. One says, in effect, that the path toward greatness that he inscribes is hardly worth the bother. One recoils at the notion of submission, understanding intuitively that this is the sworn enemy of a self bent on greatness. Those who crave the winner's circle live beholden to another Lord.

They despise Jesus' path to greatness, preferring their own devices, and so fall short in his estimation.

Instead of greatness as compared with others, we would do well to practice kindness toward others. Kindness is one of those care-full words, loaded with possibility and brimming with good. Kindness promotes and is characteristic of the community that happens among "persons bound together by the acts through which they express their common faithfulness to the Person who loves them."[6] Community emerges as people rigorously devote themselves to the labor of love, expressing themselves in various kindly ways. The group becomes characterized by kindness fueled by joy in the Lord and his prescription for life together.

Kindness tills ground compacted by competition. It cuts away at the errors that spread like zebra mussels through the pools of small groups and local churches: the focus on work over an interest in workmates; the yearning for ecstatic, spiritual experience more than simpler, often messier encounters with neighbors or colleagues; the unquestioning reception of pithy sayings; the deep-seated, culturally acceptable disdain for the poor; the fear of or revulsion toward the sick. In this, kindness enhances the community. Remember Jesus as he began to wash the feet of the disciples? Taking up the basin and towel, Jesus simply, kindly served men whose labors and journeys had left them tired and dirty. Peter protested, eager to put Jesus in his proper place. But Jesus' act meant instead to shut the mouths of those seeking greatness, because that pursuit was inherently destructive and antithetical to the program he presented.

We encounter, for instance, the problem of personal fiefdoms when each of us, committed to greatness, fashions our own kingdom. This happens individually and at times among small groups—local churches, mission agencies, parachurch organizations. We get to acting like no one else is near or competent. On the web we rule our own domains, like lords, with pages. We forget that we are meant to be members of one body rather than independently operating body parts. In Ephesians Paul asserts that this body is meant to be a unity—"There is one body," he says (4:4). The phrase is not a war cry or an invitation to displace all others, but a simple definition: We are one, and we are linked to Jesus, the head. One cannot "win" in this body and be above all other members; the only possibilities are incorporation or separation.

Then we find the way that straining toward greatness disrupts contentment. The pond changes, or the fish, and we rarely take delight in simply swimming around. Upon comparison, we discover that we are frightfully average and maddeningly acquainted with those who are luckier; we rapidly discover that even for the most successful tycoon there comes a dwarfing, a placing, a sudden realization that in the grand scheme of things, even all one has ain't so great. So we stumble in a fog. We want to be great but find ourselves likely to occupy small worlds, and we feel disappointment as their walls draw even closer. When this happens we lose delight in any accomplishment, and dissatisfaction becomes our dominant character trait. It's a situation described in excruciating detail by Solomon in Ecclesiastes, a book about learning contentment with the life God lays before us rather than striving after elusive desires.

God alone cures the smallness our passion for greatness masks; he helps us to see how that interest is so shortsighted. When we strive for greatness, we may achieve a momentary prominence, much like the moon eclipsing the sun, but very quickly the enormous living fire emerges to shine on all who turn their faces toward him. When we look out, up, around and see—really see—then we begin to achieve our true stature. We take our rightful place before God and with others. Now our whole world starts to grow because we are no longer only in a space of our own making. We move in his realm now, and it is huge.

The greatness of God is the cure for small worlds. By nature we seek our own advantage, telling ourselves stories, dreaming glorious dreams, believing that the others around us are there only for the purpose of our own satisfaction. In this we become functional solipsists, people who pursue independence and individuality to their logical conclusion. But God is too big for solipsism to persist. He shines through the small chinks in those walls we build, and like light focused through a camera's lens, he makes an impression far larger than that little hole. Indeed, his very brilliance can enlarge that hole, melting the walls to the point that the fiefdom we have so carefully erected soon lies in tatters at our feet.

The greatness of me melts in the heat of the greatness of God. The table of the Lord looms before us, ready to swallow the pride that seeks to vault us over those nearby; our mouths drop open at the enormity of what we see here. This is no amble over the prairie but a blinding encounter with the one great God. You must pull up short, dismount, and leave your aspirations at the door. There is a basin waiting, and a towel; bread, wine. And the Lord of the feast, standing there, smiling. "You're not great at all," he says. "But I am." What a relief.

Eleven

They Sang a Hymn

A spread table, heavy with food. Soul-deep conversation. Night sky pouring in at every chink. Muffled murmurs and random shouts filtering up from streets below and homes nearby. The only clock in this room is a calendar, measuring time not in minutes but with centuries. Time is passing without hurry, filled like a cup with wine—rich, sweet, and rough in the throat. The meal is drawing to a close, most every morsel consumed. Diners pull back, contented. The only thing left is a song.

It is drawn from the *Hallel,* a collection of four psalms (115–118). We know this word, *hallel,* from our own songs that use *hallelujah:* praise *(hallel)* God *(jah).* These psalms offer praise, as a quick scan of their lyrics attests. More to the point, though, is that from these psalms praise is *rendered;* from boiling vats something new and good is distilled and drawn out. Each echoes a people pressed; each wrings praise from beneath a heavy load. Former slaves may have left Egypt, but they have not yet left the planet or broken free from the wiles of neighbors or of their own hearts. Daily life brings a boatload of trouble to which one must make reply.

One can run, or hide, or ignore. One can grow brittle and bitter. One can become sick, or miserable, or malicious, or spiteful. One can render praise. Song after a meal like this is part of tradition, yes; the ancestors have always sung. But more than this. We sing because we must—in the face of this life that threatens to flatten us, we must burst forth in song or be buried by the onslaught. The *Hallel* lifts us into the realm of God, where what we need to be true can be found. By singing we affirm, declare, yield, reach, hope.

TO YOUR NAME BE THE GLORY!
Psalm 115:1

The keenest temptation when trouble comes is to turn inward, to marshal one's resources, to circle the wagons. The press of difficulty—from the word *press* we build compress, oppress, suppress—threatens to make us small and hard and timid. A parent dies, a spouse runs off, a boss bellows, a neighbor gossips—how will you deal with such pressure? How will you bear this weight? A twelve-year-old boy lost his mother unexpectedly one afternoon to sickness; we announced her death at that evening's service. Two women in the congregation spoke about it later; each, at age thirteen, had seen her mother die. "This boy needs us," they said. "Needs God."

Is it right to mention God in the same breath as disaster? Is it not more likely that he has been the cause—judging, vindictive, or ignorant? So claim those who do not dig deeply enough; they bring God in at the last moment to stand trial for what they do not comprehend. "Where was God?" they ask. "Why would he not intervene?"

The psalmist totters on the brink of disaster with eyes lifted above the shaking ground. *You*, says the psalm writer, speaking to God, not me. What is happening here is bigger than me, large enough to swallow me whole. If I insist on seeing only myself, only my situation—if I demand an accounting, a *reason* for this—I will stay at the center of this depressing storm, thinking of and caring for little else other than me. But *you* are bigger. Larger than this problem or this pressure; larger even than me. To your name—not mine—be the glory.

YOU WHO FEAR HIM, TRUST IN THE LORD.
Psalm 115:11

"How many times do I have to tell you . . . ?" begins the litany familiar to so many parents towering over their errant children. Kids forget, and we who parent them get exasperated. "But I *told* you," we say. "Remember?" Hmmm. Reach into your own brain and heart: Can you recall something you forgot, some advice you didn't take, some rule you ignored, some behavior you avoided? We forgive ourselves so easily for such lapses, but the fact remains that we forget, too, and often we forget what is vitally important. Like trusting God. How often has he proved himself faithful? How regularly do we assume that this time will be different? How routine is it that when we face a crisis we are paralyzed by fear or enraged by discomfort? Phrases so frequent they have become almost hackneyed emerge then, like "trust God." How trite, we might think. Then, how true. The psalmists do not tire of repeating the well known. They seem to see children in their audience who need those patient reminders so that the life worth living can be continued with a series of gentle prods.

I WAS OVERCOME BY TROUBLE AND SORROW. . . . OUR GOD IS FULL OF COMPASSION.
Psalm 116:3, 5

To judge from so many of our stories, sorrow often shines most intensely, casting compassion in deep shadow. Why is it this way and not the reverse? Perhaps we prefer pain too often, finding in it grounds for laying blame at another's feet. Perhaps many of us are gripped by what G. K. Chesterton called a "metaphysical doubt."[1] But Passover helps us through this morass, acknowledging the sorrow of slaves and then trumpeting the compassion of a savior. "I will lift up the cup of salvation," says this psalm writer, "and call on the name of the LORD" (v. 13). No interminable wallowing in what is truly troubling here, but rather another fiercely determined look above circumstances to see the One who comes to save.

PRAISE THE LORD, ALL YOU NATIONS; EXTOL HIM, ALL YOU PEOPLES. FOR GREAT IS HIS LOVE TOWARD US, AND THE FAITHFULNESS OF THE LORD ENDURES FOREVER. PRAISE THE LORD.
Psalm 117

In the center of the *Hallel* stands this double affirmation of "Praise the LORD." There is little more than this in the shortest of all psalms, but it is a fitting phrase to find. Why praise him? Because of his great love for us, because he is faithful even when we are distracted and indifferent.

GIVE THANKS TO THE LORD, FOR HE IS GOOD; HIS LOVE ENDURES FOREVER.
Psalm 118:1, repeated in verse 29

This much longer psalm is also bound on both ends by a single refrain, and within those "bookends" is a litany of reasons for thanksgiving. It sounds like what people should sing after a fine meal and good stories. This psalm is a conscious, albeit metaphorical, retelling of the Exodus, complete with memories of threats, battles, provision, and festivities. Buzzing armies are put to rest (v. 12); the rock-littered wilderness through which the people wandered evokes the image of one great stone on which a nation can be built (v. 22).

I WILL NOT DIE BUT LIVE.
Psalm 118:17

Jesus, the One who passes bread and cup among disciples about to run from him, has been speaking for years about death. In this very meal he has referred directly to his own imminent demise. The song on the lips of all who celebrate Passover raises as a vivid declaration the expectation of immortality: death may visit, but life will prevail! As they came to this line in the lyric, might those disciples have suddenly paused, gripped by a new insight? As they pondered the cross, visited the tomb,

147

suddenly found Jesus among them some days later, might this phrase have exploded with unexpected meaning?

YOU ARE MY GOD, AND I WILL GIVE YOU THANKS;
YOU ARE MY GOD, AND I WILL EXALT YOU.
Psalm 118:28

Are disciples eyeing the table for leftovers or gazing out the window at this point in the *Hallel?* Or are they like Peter, who when asked first about popular opinion and then for his own opinion concerning Jesus blurts, "You are the Christ!" Are they like Peter, suddenly illumined by the One at table with them now? They will go with him to the Garden and Jesus will agonize there, entangled by the cords of death, overwhelmed by the anguish of the grave, creased by trouble and sorrow (Ps. 116:3). They will be overcome with sleep; they will later run like scared rabbits and stay burrowed out of sight; and then, after the Lord's resurrection, they too will emerge from the dark, indomitable. The bold declaration of the psalmist taken up by generations of Passover singers acquires new weight and power for those who stand before and look upon the Lord.

They sang a hymn. Why? For many reasons. When people gather to eat, celebrate, even invade, it is not unusual for song to break out; deep matters of the heart surface with music. This is certainly one way of accounting for the role music plays in worship. We might spend a lot of time analyzing the sort of songs to be sung[2] or, more profitably, simply notice that songs have always had a place in the community of faith. David, from whom so many psalms emerge, knits singing into the

148

nation's life and celebration; his example is followed ever after. But songs have an earlier root. There is, for instance, the musical work of Moses and Miriam on the far side of the Red Sea as they watch Pharaoh and his hordes flounder in the rushing water. Their song enters the scrapbook of Jacob's children, to be pulled out often when life gets hard. We may have an even older referent, describing a completely different realm for worship, in a poetic report of the morning stars' singing at creation (Job 38:7).[3]

Songs give us language for expressing the nature of God and his activity among people, the condition of a heart bursting with joy or laden by despair. Martin Luther set theology to music so the illiterate could express their convictions and engage in the conversation; Charles Wesley did much the same to accompany and amplify his brother John's reasoned sermons. We sense in our hearts that rhetoric, as good as it can be, is insufficient and only occasionally addresses the whole person. Music, presented in all its kaleidoscopic variety, does this routinely.[4]

Why do we sing? To prepare us for something yet to come. Recently some older women of faith in the web of my relationships died. Their health had been failing, and as their ends neared, friends and family gathered to watch and wait with them. Doctors came and went, medicines were administered, procedures were done, and systemic failures began to occur. The knot of the living drew tighter, and this is what emerged: song. Hymns and choruses old and new came out to fill rooms like incense. The restive grew still and the semi-comatose smiled at such times; something beyond science was afoot. People sing in the face of death. The songs they choose are reverent, evocative of deep and precious memories. These songs, lodged in the hearts of faithful worshipers, touch places microscopes could not find. They pave a path for what lies ahead, still unmapped.

Why sing? The answer depends on who is asked. A musician, for instance, will give you a quizzical look; musicians sing like artists paint and professors mull and outfielders shag: this is what we do, who we are. Non-musicians are less likely to be passionate about singing, although they are often very particular about their music. And while they are frequently shy about being heard, they will often belt out Broadway tunes or pop songs or even church music when alone. Why?

We sing, in part, because we can. Of all God's creatures humans alone sing. Other animals make noise to be sure, some of which sounds wonderfully close to music. But listen carefully and realize that even the most glorious songbird or sonorous whale has a profoundly limited repertoire. Humans, on the other hand, produce an ever-expanding songbook. We delight in the virtuosity and variety and sheer familiarity of music; we break out in song at odd moments and include singing as part of solemn occasions. We sing because we recognize in music a delightful gift we are eager to enjoy.

Songs linger. They seep into us and stay. We welcome music into our lives, notice its absence. It is emotional more than rational; we esteem singers and songwriters, hang on what they have to say to us, imitate their ways. Our songs come from all over. The "music industry" thrives in Brazil, post-communist Russia, and Kansas; headphones have become ubiquitous while a new generation of hand-crank electronic devices insures that even in remote areas where there is no reliable electricity, the sounds that move people can still be played. When "they sang a hymn," these disciples entered a stream that had washed their ancestors and would bathe their progeny. Their song refreshed their souls, splashed their imaginations, and lubricated their memories.

They sang a hymn. Whether all or part of Psalms 115 to 118, the body of music these disciples tapped into on its surface expressed the praise of a redeemed community and deeper down recognized the darker forces still at work. Songs—sung poetry—do this especially well, blending pathos and ecstasy, fusing mind and heart. In the *Hallel* we praise the God who hears our anguished cries; we thank our generous God, mindful of how bankrupt we had become. The song stirs memory and pricks the mind with a second sight: The One deserving praise is he who moves inexorably towards the altar of sacrifice (Ps. 118:27). Death is just steps away. But we do not cower in its face; rather we move with the One nearing it, pulled in ever closer, finding within us the urge to say "thank you" and to give praise. We sing because we have been given the means for expressing what mere words cannot quite achieve, and in the singing we find the joy of contact with places our minds only faintly knew.

The disciples' parents had done this, and their parents before them, and their parents back to the earliest survivors of Egyptian domination. A new Lord emerged for them then, the One true Lord of their own ancestors, whose story had fallen into the mud pits and been trampled with the straw. Now this Lord was on the move—and the poets would set his exploits to song. These songs would pass like treasured heirlooms from generation to generation; songs do this. These songs would spill out over kneading bowls and during harvests and always at Passover, seizing hearts and catching fire in brains; songs do this, too. When the nation paused for its annual holiday, it had a menu and a soundtrack, and both warmed the soul and stirred the imagination.

They sang a hymn because it was a fitting finale to a night of memory and anticipation; song was a part of the larger ritual, an element of the sacrament. Already bread and wine were pointing people to something more than food. Now in song, mere words lifted souls to something beyond communication.[5] They sang as part of a well-crafted, familiar script and in singing rose beyond any common ritual. This is sacramental: physical things pushing us into the spiritual realm. With this hymn, they put their whole selves into worship, as we can and do.

Twelve

Table Grace

We came to probe its mystery, to reduce this land to
  terms of science,
But there is always the indefinable which holds aloof
  yet rivets our souls.

Douglas Mawson[1]

The king of Aram was plotting his latest raid against
Israel (see 2 Kings 6:8–23). Aram, the land we know
today as Syria, lived in long-standing tension with their
southern neighbors, and previous campaigns against
them had been largely victorious. This newest attack
should have been simply one more for the plus column;
without doubt it would be another successful corporate
takeover, a fresh opportunity to stroke egos and inflict
pain. Instead, plans went awry. There was a spy in the
ranks, one who could report what this king said in private. What to do?

The king investigates and learns that the "spy" is a
prophet named Elisha, living in the very land he intends
to conquer. So he assembles a "strong force" tasked with

routing this threat; this Aramean king will not brook interruptions of his intentions. One night his troops surround Dothan, the city where Elisha is staying, and at daybreak, the prophet's servant wakes to see the soldiers, horses, and chariots. He doesn't need to count; he knows they are overmatched. "What shall we do?" he cries (v. 15).

Elisha, unperturbed, prays that the servant's eyes will be open wide enough to see the Lord's forces arrayed in protection and then that the eyes of the enemy soldiers would be shut. Sight comes, and blindness, and more, for Elisha will lead these soldiers on a day's walk from Dothan to Samaria, a city of Israel the Arameans had conquered before. There the blinded men receive vision only to discover that they are deep in hostile territory. The king of Israel is waiting for them with his own strong force, ready to slay the foreigners. "Do not kill them," Elisha directs (v. 22). Rather he tells the king to set a table and bring them food and drink. The king does this: he prepares a "great feast" which the Arameans eat. We are left to imagine their conversation around that table; all we know is that after the meal they left and "the bands from Aram stopped raiding Israel's territory" (v. 23).

We check our charts, test the winds, think carefully or launch from the gut, and march out boldly in pursuit of our next conquest, knowing without doubt the outcome. We will expand our territory, improve our standing, shore up our confidence, acquire bragging rights, flex our muscles, whistle in the dark. We have Aramean genes, or Laodicean—those with a family crest that reads: "I am rich; I have acquired wealth and do not need a thing" (Rev. 3:17). We are blinded by our own ambition.

"What do you see?" The Lord asks this of Jeremiah at the outset of that prophet's ministry (Jer. 1:11). Jeremiah, "one of the priests at Anathoth" (1:1), already knows what it means to be in the Lord's service. Now he is being asked about further usefulness: Can he see clearly enough to discern what the Lord is up to? It is a question for all today who seek to live in the kingdom of God; vision is not, despite current emphasis to the contrary, important only for the leaders among us. Each follower of Jesus is expected to see clearly, having been offered sight by the Lord.

Seeing is important. Just ask the person who has worn thick glasses since kindergarten or one with the cloudy cataracts of age or infirmity. Why? It's practical: sight helps us manage life. It's aesthetic, too: there is simply so much to look at. Jesus knows the importance of accurate vision; at the outset of his public ministry, he announced that he had come to open eyes:

> The Spirit of the Lord is upon me,
> because he has anointed me
> to preach good news to the poor.
> He has sent me to proclaim freedom for the prisoners,
> and recovery of sight for the blind.
>
> Luke 4:18

The Gospels' stories of Jesus tell us how he healed those blind from birth, physically and spiritually; he appeared like a comet, both bright and expected, and "those walking in darkness [saw] a great light" (Matt.

155

4:16).[2] Envisioned in these terms, Jesus is all about helping people—like randy Arameans or self-important Laodiceans—exposing them to what is necessary, true, and good. Jesus wants people to see what is going on. The table of communion is a good example of this. Look carefully. Stare at this simple surface as though seeing your child, lover, or friend after a long absence. Look as though you had laid eyes on a treasure long sought. Look as though you had been blind for years and suddenly had your vision restored.

See first the Lord, high and lifted up, to recall Isaiah again, as his train filled the temple. Peer over John's shoulder, as he stood one day on Patmos, at the voice coming from one who was shining. Your first response should not be to lick your lips in anticipation of a meal but to fall to your knees in awe before the One revealing himself afresh. God is here. We do not need to invoke his presence so much as to pray for awareness; we must take care that he does not get covered by our particular concerns or obfuscated by the equipment of the service. God is central, high and exalted, the consuming fire who can blaze like an inferno or smolder like charcoal in burning away all that warrants removal from our lives. So look at him, and come not as those planning to dig in and pig out but as people about to be consumed, for the One who calls wants people to lose themselves in him.[3]

See next the Host, who has set this table and who welcomes to it now as honored guests those previously estranged from him on account of sin. That is what hospitality entails—the opening of hearth and home to the distant and undeserving—and it is precisely what Jesus has done. "I'm going to prepare a place for you," he had taught, "and I will return to take you there. You will be with me then, even as I call you to join me now."[4] This is the One Paul knew—Paul, that self-confident warrior of the faith who was suddenly blinded on his way into Syria. Led by the hand to a place he did not know, Paul could only have expected to receive what he was so eager to dole out. Instead he is met by grace and given his sight and a place at the table.

See this table not just as a place to dump books, pile paper, or slam down a few plates before embarking on your next great adventure. See it like the kid in this photo in your mind: She is little and tanned, surrounded by a doting family. Her mother is holding a birthday cake inches from her face, which is split wide with a smile. Many are gathered at this festive holiday table; everyone is grinning like pumpkins. The food is wonderful, the company superb, the air electric. We would come to a table like that. The Lord's Passover fades to the background as the Lord's Table assumes prominence; people once as blind as turnips approach with eyes open, and minds, and hearts. Here we feel the cross against our skin, wince at fist and thorn, stop our ears against the moans, swat flies and smell death, and then look through all that to the power of life blowing stone doors off a new grave. At this banquet table, all of a sudden we notice how hungry we are; it's been forever since we had a decent meal in a peaceful setting.

Finally see the bread and cup, which remind people who have a palpable longing for what is spiritual that only what is truly of the Spirit can satisfy. They point us to grace and provoke those who look to ponder grace, to ingest and imbibe it. We are not done with grace once we pass the "point" of salvation; we are not yet safe enough.

As Hebrews pleads, people with sight restored by faith should "approach the throne of grace with confidence, so that we may receive mercy and find grace to help us in our time of need" (Heb. 4:16).

Communion does not so much convey grace as to show it in ways we can perceive. The Supper insists on the impact and operation of grace and encourages a fresh valuing of it. We who have a street address in the suburb of human endeavor, potential, and all-around competence quickly become blind to the grace of God. So we need to move closer to the table, to have our memories refreshed by, to give thanks for, to be enriched with grace. Participating in communion is not like cleaning the oven, to be done on occasion and only when needed, as much as like learning a language. After all, we are entering a new community, and as we cross into this new culture, we will go through various stages; we will by turns be comfortable, uneasy, elated, perplexed. We will miss the old ways; we will only gradually adopt what is new.

But we can change, particularly as we come to see what is going on. We will appreciate stories, pictures, charts, tables. The Lord's Table will serve as a way station while we adapt to this new home. It will help us see more clearly and will provide the sustenance we need for life in this realm. The food here stocks us with what we need to live as he directs. We who eat are those God fills, and in whom he walks around to serve and speak; bread and wine become his flesh and blood as those who are infused by grace begin to incarnate grace.

If anything marks us off as being different from God, it is this display of grace. We can occasionally muster kindness, at times exhibit peace. But the consistent, resplendent outpouring of grace is beyond our natural ability; it's like asking a tadpole to tap dance. And yet, God thinks we can and should. He comes close enough to shower us in grace to the point that we start reeking of it; he tears into our chests and slathers grace all over our hearts. Then he says, "You do this, too." You who have been saved by grace and who in your days under his lordship have been shaped by it as well—you are also to show grace.

But how do you do what does not come naturally? Watch the gymnast, flautist, or welder. To do something new and different and so fundamentally out of natural character, two things are necessary: You need practice. You need exposure.

To show grace, you need to practice faithfulness and loyalty; you need to put yourself out not once or twice but times without counting. It happens in small ways and large, in fits and starts. You drive and spend and listen and help until you are out of breath, until your fingers bleed, until you are broken and torn apart. This sounds implausible, impossible almost, but there is no easy way to say it, because grace is good, not simple. So you watch dear ones make bad choices and pick them up afterwards; you take on the chin a purposeful blow and do not let it knock you for a loop. You amass a fortune and spend it lavishly. You whisper *I forgive you* and mean it.

To show grace, you need to be near grace. You have a lousy, selective, self-serving memory, too, so you will need to stay close—for more than a few minutes, or hours, or months. You will need to stare until your eyes water, you will need to set to song what you note of grace and sing until you are hoarse. You will need to eat and drink your fill of grace and then come back for more. And you will do this over and over and over again because the showing of grace will deplete you, and your only source of strength—not one of several, not a pretty good place to go, not a fine idea when you have the time, but your *only* source of strength—will be the One who poured himself out for you, who allowed his body to be pulled apart so that you could take hold.

You know from experience that self is the enemy of grace, that self blinds you to God and closes your ears to truth. So when healing grace comes, you must open your eyes and look hard; you must listen for a voice calling loud and clear, "Come and get it!" It's a command, an invitation, a promise, a relief. You will stagger to his table some days with barely enough strength to see what's there. On others you will float in, elated by what just happened to or through you. On many you will simply come, vowing to fight off the threat of boredom, probably struggling, maybe sinking, but determined to win this round. You will come because you know you need grace.[5]

And then, one day soon, you will die.

And then you will be immersed, saturated, resplendent and full of new hunger. You will raise your head and with eyes wide and shining see before you what you never deserved but what mercy brought to pass: a table loaded with the fruit of the field and vine, waiting. You will be swept along by a current of effusive praise to the mercy-giver, and glory will race around you like river rapids. In this place where you see the Lord over all, you will finally feel at home, safe and alive. You will hear your name and embrace your kin and know that grace is calling each and all of you, still.

Immanuel's Land

O Christ He is the fountain, the deep sweet well of
    love!
The streams on earth I've tasted more deep I'll drink
    above!
There, to an ocean fullness, His mercy doth expand
And glory, glory dwelleth, in Immanuel's land.

With mercy and with judgement my web of time He
    wove
And aye the dews of sorrow were lustered with His
    love
I'll bless the hand that guided, I'll bless the heart that
    planned
When throned where glory dwelleth in Immanuel's
    land.

Oh! I am my beloved's, and my beloved's mine
He brings a poor vile sinner into His house of wine!
I stand upon His merit, I know no other stand
Not e'en where glory dwelleth in Immanuel's land.

The bride eyes not her garment, but her dear Bride-
    groom's face
I will not gaze at glory, but on my King of grace
Not at the crown He giveth, but on His pierced hand
The Lamb is all the glory in Immanuel's land.

Anne Rose Cousin (1824–1906)

Notes

Introduction

1. A mentor once passed along Mary McDermott Shideler's *A Creed for a Christian Skeptic* (Grand Rapids: Eerdmans, 1968), which scrutinized the Apostles' Creed one phrase—and sometimes one word—at a time. I've borrowed that same approach here.

2. Quotations of biblical figures or writers which appear without Scripture references indicate my own conjecture about thoughts or dialogue.

Chapter 1: The Lord Jesus

1. As discussed in *The Rule of St. Benedict*, trans. Anthony C. Meisel and M. L. del Mastro (New York: Image Books, 1975).

2. Leon Morris knows that each of these has their place. He compares the Gospel of John to "a pool in which a child may wade and an elephant can swim." *The Gospel According to John* (Grand Rapids: Eerdmans, 1971), 7.

3. Tolkien's Frodo "felt in his heart that Faramir, though he was much like his brother in looks, was a man less self-regarding, both sterner and wiser." J. R. R. Tolkien, *The Two Towers* (Boston: Houghton Mifflin Company, 1965), 274.

Chapter 2: On the Night

1. The chief tool for this is the *Haggadah,* which compiles biblical portions with rabbinic commentary to guide the banquet celebration.

2. Derek Lundy, *Godforsaken Sea* (Chapel Hill: Algonquin Books, 1999), 152–58.

3. While it is not universally agreed what kind of meal Jesus and his disciples actually did have that night—the Synoptic accounts and John's Gospel seem to give conflicting reports—I take the position here that they met for

the purpose of a Passover celebration. As Anthony Thiselton concludes after an extensive survey of various positions, "the many factors customarily cited to establish a Passover framework remain utterly convincing." *The First Epistle to the Corinthians: A Commentary on the Greek Text* (Grand Rapids: Eerdmans, 2000), 871–74.

Eugene Peterson prefers to view the apparent discrepancies in other terms: "It is not necessary to decide beforehand whether the Eucharist was instituted as a replacement for (and fulfillment of) the Passover ritual (as the Synoptic accounts have it) or as a separate act which draws its symbolism and timing from the Passover event (as John describes it): in either case the Passover background is undisputed and insures liturgical and pastoral continuities for the worshiping people of God." *Five Smooth Stones for Pastoral Work* (Philadelphia: John Knox Press, 1980), 55.

4. Gerald Hawthorne perceptively and clearly shows the connection between John 13 and Philippians 2 in *Philippians*, vol. 43 of the Word Biblical Commentary (Waco: Word, 1983), 78–79.

Chapter 3: He Was Betrayed

1. To be complete, it is also true that Philip is always listed fifth and James son of Alphaeus ninth.

2. This is Ralph Martin's phrase from the *Illustrated Bible Dictionary*, part 2 (Leicester: Inter-Varsity Press, 1994), 831. Martin also points out that the Gospels do not record Judas addressing Jesus as Lord but only as "Rabbi."

3. Jude speaks negatively of "the way of Cain" (Jude 11), but this reference does not necessarily preclude a change of heart later in Cain's life.

4. Anthony Thiselton's observation bears further consideration. He notes that the Greek behind *betrayed* also translates to *handed over*, and as such may refer to action of the Father. The same verb, Thiselton observes, comes in Romans 8:32, where Paul says that God "gave him up [i.e., handed Jesus over] for us all." It may then be that we are to remember in the communion how Jesus gave himself up "voluntarily to renounce self-direction and autonomy (and) to place his selfhood and destiny in the hands of God and human persons without any further 'say' in what happens." *First Epistle to the Corinthians*, 870.

This suggests a better way of dealing with Jesus' "cry of dereliction" from the cross: "My God, my God, why have you forsaken me?" (Matt. 27:46). As commonly taken, this cry expresses the Son's anguish that the Father has turned his back. If that is the case, then God's "betrayal" is also in view during the Passion of our Lord. But it is also possible—indeed, I would say likely—that the Father has not betrayed the Son or vice versa. Instead, Jesus' plaintive cry voices the true pain he feels at bearing sin and the full brunt of God's wrath. Nonetheless, as the rest of the psalm from which this snippet comes says, God is not far when trouble is near (Ps. 22:11, 19, 24).

5. Scholars note the difficulties in reconciling Matthew's account of Judas's demise with Luke's account in Acts. While Matthew seems to indicate that

Judas hung himself immediately after Jesus' conviction by Pilate, it may also be possible that Judas lived a few more days. Paul says in 1 Corinthians 15:5 that Jesus appeared, after his resurrection, to the Twelve. Various commentators argue that this title may have only been general, referring to those of the original Twelve still remaining. But what if it is meant literally—what if Judas did see the risen Lord? For many, like Peter and Jesus' half-brothers James and Jude, such an encounter was life-changing. If Judas did see Jesus and still did not recant, his condemnation was all the more sure. Despite frequent exposure to Jesus before the arrest, despite warnings during the Supper, even with the sort of post-resurrection appearance which was re-orienting for others, Judas did not turn. He resisted God's mercy to the end.

Isaiah's comment is illustrative: "Though grace is shown to the wicked, they do not learn righteousness; even in a land of uprightness they go on doing evil and regard not the majesty of the LORD" (Isa. 26:10).

6. A person dedicated more to financial gain than honest service of the Lord might well have decided to revolt once Jesus' true intentions were made perfectly clear. In Georges Bernanos's unassuming novel *The Diary of a Country Priest*, the meek Curé de Torcy imagines Jesus addressing the pecuniary concerns of Judas after he criticized the pouring of perfume on Jesus' feet: "The weak will always be an insufferable burden on your shoulders, a dead weight which your proud civilizations will pass on to each other with rage and loathing. I have placed My mark upon their foreheads, and now you can only confront them with cringing fury; you may devour one lost sheep, but you will never again dare attack the flock." From *The Diary of a Country Priest* (New York: Image Books, 1962), 49.

7. The writer of Hebrews encourages Jesus' followers to recall his example in the face of opposition so that they might be courageous when trouble comes (12:3).

Chapter 4: This Loaf, This Cup

1. The "bread from heaven" to which Jesus refers reminds his listeners of the story recorded in Exodus 16, which describes Israel's children shortly after God had dispatched Pharaoh and his troops at the Red Sea. Despite this recent, vivid miracle, the people challenged Moses, whined about God, and voiced their interest in returning to Egypt. "We're hot, tired, hungry," they said.

So God sent food. He explained himself one evening, and then the next morning there came a white dusting of the earth, sparkling crystals that looked like frost. The people, emerging from their tents, couldn't believe their eyes: frost in the desert? They bent to examine, scooped flakes from the rocks and twigs, put fragments on to their tongues. It was sweet, like honey. What is it? they wondered. *Mah*, the Hebrew interrogative; *nah*, a Hebrew relative pronoun. *Manna*—what's this? Bread from heaven, they concluded. God came through.

The initial provision of manna was intended to satisfy daily needs; manna had a distinctly temporary nature, as those who tried to keep extra even overnight discovered to their dismay. But God also wanted the evidence of his provision to remain in clear view, and so had Moses and Aaron fill a jar with the stuff to be "kept for the generations to come" (Exod. 16:33).

2. Markus Barth points out that in Scripture the phrase "body and blood" routinely refers to a life—typically of an animal—given or about to be given as a sacrifice. See, for example, page 61 in *Rediscovering the Lord's Supper* (Atlanta: John Knox Press, 1988).

3. It's a small point, perhaps, but among those who take the verb literally, the tendency is to give it a future cast. That is, few if any give *is* a truly *present* sense, which would imply that when Jesus and the others arrived at the upper room for their meal, the loaf and wine were already—indeed had been from their inception—the body and blood of Jesus. The overwhelming majority favoring the literal slant take "is" to mean "will become."

4. Gordon Fee, looking also at 1 Corinthians 10:4 and Galatians 4:25, says that "as in all such identifications, Jesus means 'this signifies/represents my body.'" *First Epistle to the Corinthians*, New International Commentary of the New Testament (Grand Rapids: Eerdmans, 1987), 550. Markus Barth takes a different tack, concluding that "at the Lord's table, the words 'This is . . .' are the beginning of a statement about why his disciples are to continue meeting at his table, not about the substance of the food." *Rediscovering the Lord's Supper* (Atlanta: John Knox Press, 1988), 16.

5. Scanning a wide field of religious thought and practice, Thomas Cahill remarks that "all sacrifices, even the communion bread, must be set aside and somehow broken, consumed or transformed in order to be authentic. This is part of the 'logic' of sacrifice." *How the Irish Saved Civilization* (New York: Doubleday, 1995), 142.

6. This is the perspective of Hebrews 8:8, which explains that the new covenant was made because "God found fault with the people" who bailed out of the earlier agreement.

7. That is, God does not keep doing exactly the same thing endlessly with each generation, but introduces new methods and information along the way.

8. Jeremiah looks ahead to describe God's unfolding plan when he predicts a new covenant to replace what Israel had broken (31:31–34). Ezekiel anticipates a time when God's people will have hearts finally soft to him (11:19–20; 36:26–28). Zechariah includes a wonderful promise of deliverance that is precipitated by "the blood of my [i.e., God's] covenant" (Zech. 9:11).

9. Matthew, Mark, and Luke all include Jesus' statement about his blood being poured out "for many" (Matthew and Mark) or "for you" (Luke). This "pouring" is common to "sacrifice" language: "a libation completes any offering made to God." Hawthorne, *Philippians*, 106. Paul does not refer to the pouring, perhaps because he writes to people whose presence in the kingdom is a vivid illustration of the fulfillment of Jesus' promise; he knows

the sacrifice has been made and sees ample evidence of its effect in the churches he addresses.

10. It's rewarding to unpack the metaphorical sense of bread and wine even further. Consider, for instance:

a) By the simple fact that in communion as we eat and drink we indicate our dependency within the created order. However, this does not suggest that we are simply on par with the rest of what God has made; as Wendell Berry says, our responsibility is to "keep Creation's neighborhood." *A Timbered Choir* (Washington, D.C.: Counterpoint, 1998), 190.

b) The multisensory nature of both and what implications that might have for worship. For a look at ruminations on the deeper significance of bread, see Peter Reinhart, *Brother Juniper's Bread Book: Slow Rise as Method and Metaphor* (New York: Aris Books, 1991), and Robert Capon, *The Supper of the Lamb: A Culinary Reflection* (New York: Doubleday, 1969). Here's a nugget from Reinhart: "a little yeast raises the whole loaf and it does it in a sacrificial manner, for, once its mission has been completed, it must die in order for the loaf to live" (p. 22).

c) The way "things are here to immerse us in the sacred." Gina Bria, reflecting on the nature of "things," examines the material world from a theological perspective. "We are meant to have a relationship with things," she says, noting that this relationship allows things to "do their telling work." Things provoke memory, and while memory can make us wistful, the loss we feel upon recollection "only tells us that we have read our condition correctly, we are indeed living in a lost world and await its retrieval." She warns that "things do not have magical powers. Rather, they have theological powers, and that is what we want to take hold of in this life, and . . . the next. Recognizing this power is the beginning of incarnational living." Finally, she affirms that the "more our senses are engaged, the more realistic [an] object can claim to be. God gave us our senses to find and enjoy Him." "A Theology of Things," *Mars Hill Review*, no. 10 (1998): 9–12.

Chapter 5: He Gave Thanks

1. This paraphrases Ephesians 1:12, where the NIV has Paul addressing people who put hope in Christ and "might be for the praise of his glory." If the verb translated here as *be* is understood as *exist,* we have in this verse a "purpose statement" for Christian life.

2. The other is *euloge.* In their accounts, Matthew and Mark each use *euloge* once and *eucharist* once; Luke has *eucharist* twice.

3. Henri Nouwen notices in the Eucharist celebration "a movement . . . from resentment to gratitude." *With Burning Hearts: A Meditation on the Eucharistic Life* (Maryknoll, N.Y.: Orbis Books, 1994), 13.

4. A very early Christian document, *The Didache,* is replete with prayers of thanksgiving in its treatment of the Eucharist. Writing near the middle of the second century, Justin Martyr in his First Apology mentions the "copious thanks" offered by those who lead communion in the community.

Chapter 6: Remember

1. Gordon Fee points out the significance of the immediate context for understanding Paul's teaching on the Supper in his fine commentary *First Epistle to the Corinthians*, 557–67. His work also shows how this section is linked with Paul's teaching in 1 Corinthians 10:16–22 and deals with the other correctives in this epistle.

2. "Prone to Wander," Chris Rice, © 1997 by Clumsy Fly Music (Administered by Word Music, Inc.). All rights reserved. Used by permission.

3. From "A Penitential Order: Rite One," *The Book of Common Prayer* (1979), 320.

4. Conclusion of "A Penitential Order: Rite One," from *The Book of Common Prayer*.

5. Father Lorenzo Albacete reflects that confession "is not therapy, nor is it moral accounting. At its best, it is the affirmation that the ultimate truth of our interior life is our absolute poverty, our radical dependence, our unquenchable thirst, our desperate need to be loved." "Secrets of the Confessional," *New York Times Magazine*, 7 May 2000, 120.

Chapter 7: Whenever You Eat and Drink

1. I. H. Marshall says Paul's account differs from those of the Gospels because he "is concerned with the institution of the Lord's Supper," while they record the Last Supper. *Commentary on Luke*, New International Greek Testament Commentary (Grand Rapids: Eerdmans, 1978), 804. Paul's comment is also another indicator of how this meal differs from Passover. "Whenever" is ambiguous in contrast to the fixed schedule of that festival's annual celebration.

2. Indeed, we may do well to revise our notion of "seeker-sensitivity" by considering again that God is the One who seeks. What does it mean to be sensitive to *him?*

3. From the earliest times, the church has agreed that participation with the bread and cup is for people of faith, typically those already baptized. What I suggest here is not that we relax that standard, but that we welcome all those God has drawn to gatherings for worship and expect that all will be confronted with the reality of Jesus as on display in the elements of communion. It is likely, if such emphasis be placed, that some accustomed to participating in communion will be newly challenged about the condition of their faith and that those new to such gatherings will, for the first time, eat and drink with understanding and gratitude.

Congregations that offer communion often generally introduce that portion of the service with explanations and even respectful warnings along these lines: "The table before us takes us back to the cross, where Jesus died on behalf of sinners. By eating the bread and drinking from the cup, one admits one's need for that sacrificial death and further testifies to a connection with the Lord who rose after death. If you're not ready to make that sort of affirmation, you can refrain from participating today and instead use the time to reflect on this story. Might it be describing something you wish were true? It may be that you'll receive communion for the first time with new insight—that you'll recognize that this is not a snack during a long service or something one does simply by virtue of being 'in church.' And it may be that as you eat and drink, you will be freshly, deeply aware of God's love and grace and that thanks for what he has done, is doing, and has yet to do will flow from your grateful heart."

4. Luke gives a good summary of Christian experience and influence in Acts 4.

5. Is it significant that we often *do* set expensive TVs and stereos atop particular furniture and give vast quantities of time and attention to them?

6. Henri Blocher points out that the widespread desire for liberty is dangerous. He recalls that "liberty" comes from a Latin root; Liber was the Roman god of chaos. *In the Beginning* (Downers Grove, Ill.: InterVarsity Press, 1984), 72.

7. Quoting Aidan Kavanaugh, Kathleen Norris shows how the discipline of gathering for worship, for example, "gives time for theological reflection." *The Cloister Walk* (New York: Riverhead Books, 1996), 61. Introducing her book, Norris notes, "In our culture, time can seem like an enemy: it chews us up and spits us out with appalling ease. But the monastic perspective welcomes time as a gift from God, and seeks to put it to good use rather than allowing us to be used up by it" (xix).

8. Dillard introduces a wide cast of characters during her reflections on how life gets spent [*For the Time Being* (New York: Alfred A. Knopf, 1999)]. She quotes Teilhard repeatedly, as here: "'Throughout my whole life,' he noted later, 'during every minute of it, the world has been gradually lighting up and blazing before my eyes until it has come to surround me, entirely lit up from within'" (13).

9. "Speed is the enemy of the ethical preparation and eating of food. It dishonors food and it dishonors us. We have to *make* time for our food." Alice Waters, "Happy Meals," *Utne Reader*, May–June 2002, 59.

Chapter 8: You Proclaim the Lord's Death

1. The topic of evangelism is enormous and well-served by good resources. Here I deal with only a small slice of a larger pie by considering some of the gospel's content. Delivery of that information calls for more than mastery of a single "approach"; it's more like painting a sunset than landing a plane. Brian McLaren notices this when he encourages conversation instead of conversion; see his *More Ready Than You Realize* (Grand Rapids: Zondervan, 2002).

2. "The Lord's Supper is not simply a memorial of the Last Supper, nor of Christ's death per se. It is a constant, repeated reminder—and experience—of the efficacy of that death for us." Fee, *First Epistle to the Corinthians*, 558.

3. This story is quoted and edited, with permission, from e-mail correspondence.

4. As the Hebrew text prefaces Psalm 90.

5. Paul's honest appraisal in 2 Corinthians 5:1–10 warrants meditation in this regard.

6. So says Dietrich Bonhoeffer. A few years after Bonhoeffer was hanged in Germany, a young college student near Chicago wrote in his journal, "God, I pray light these idle sticks of my life and may I burn up for Thee. Consume my life, my God, for it is Thine. I seek not a long life but a full one, like Yours, Lord Jesus." *The Journals of Jim Elliot*, ed. Elisabeth Elliot (Old Tappan, N.J.: Revell, 1978), 18.

7. St. Benedict lists seventy-two "instruments of good works," which he further describes as "the tools of our spiritual craft." Number forty-seven on the list is this: "to see death before us daily." *The Rule of St. Benedict*, trans. Anthony C. Meisel and M. L. del Mastro (New York: Image Books: 1975), 52–54.

8. In some way, communicants' proclamations also make an impact on "unseen observers," those denizens of the spiritual realm which, according to apostolic teaching (see Eph. 3:10; Col. 2:15; 1 Peter 1:12), take an active interest in human affairs.

9. This is Paul's assertion in Romans 16:25.

Chapter 9: Until He Comes

1. This "kingdom talk" fits with the rest of Jesus' prominent teaching about the new realm he invited people to join. He was a king doing advance work after his first advent; in the upper room, he reminded twelve that he would soon be back to make good on all those preparations.

2. Abbot Sisois answered a concerned brother like this: "Commit yourself entirely to God. Any evil that comes to you, confess that it has happened to you because of your sins, for you must learn to attribute everything to the dispensation of God's wisdom." Sisois's remark is one of those attributed to various desert fathers and collected by Thomas Merton in *The Wisdom of the Desert* (New York: New Directions Publishing Company, 1960), 38.

3. Merton, *Wisdom of the Desert*, 8. Walter Brueggemann adds that the "community at the margin, when it functions at all, is a community of intense, trustful waiting." *Cadences of Home: Preaching Among Exiles* (Louisville: Westminster John Knox Press, 1997), 105.

4. Paul routinely argues that Christian living should be motivated by Christ's sacrifice. He makes this teaching explicit in places like Romans 6 and Colossians 3.

Chapter 10: Who Is the Greatest?

1. One prophet quotes God: "Who despises the day of small things?" (Zech. 4:10). It's a penetrating question for those enmeshed by cultures that proffer ever-increasing doses of excitement and spectacle in movies, theme parks, and even restaurants. Jesus' later words about mustard seeds—small things that yield great good—are further indications about the Lord's values.

2. She is quoted by Kathleen Norris in *The Cloister Walk*, 76.

3. Antony had come to Paul, a noted recluse, to learn from the acknowledged master. After some time in conversation, the two saw a crow that "deposited a whole loaf before their wondering eyes. . . . And when they had given thanks to God, they sat down beside the margin of the crystal spring. But now sprang up a contention between them as to who should break the bread . . . Paul insisting on the right of the guest, Antony countering by right of seniority. At length they agreed that each should take hold of the loaf and pull toward himself." St. Jerome, "The Life of St. Paul the First Hermit," trans. Helen Waddell, *The Desert Fathers* (Ann Arbor: University of Michigan Press, 1972), 35.

4. "The sin of resentment that flares up so quickly in the fellowship indicates again and again how much false desire for honor, how much unbelief, still smolders in the community." Dietrich Bonhoeffer, *Life Together* (New York: Harper & Row, 1954), 96.

5. Ibid., 107.

6. Shideler, *A Creed for a Christian Skeptic*, 141. A little later, in the same vein, Shideler says that it is "only by associating with others that the individual can achieve and preserve a sense of proportion" (145).

Chapter 11: They Sang a Hymn

1. G. K. Chesterton is but one of many examples among prominent writers and thinkers who have struggled with a pessimistic outlook. Frederick Buechner writes about Chesterton's early melancholy and traces through his writing a clear change upon the realization that "Christianity is the last, best hope for humankind." *Speak What We Feel* (San Francisco: HarperSan-Francisco, 2001), 122.

2. A lot of this goes on around us. And so we have, for example, a heated discussion on the nature of, and differences between, "psalms, hymns and spiritual songs" (Col. 3:16). Such analysis leads some to rank "church" music, according last place to more contemporary musical entries (i.e., "spiritual songs"). Others take from such a reference justification for creating such contemporary music. But what if Paul isn't attempting a description of the type of music present in (or acceptable to) the church as much as he is simply referring to the fact that the church sings? Indeed, that Matthew calls a "hymn" what clearly came from Psalms is enough to confuse the whole matter altogether.

3. This remark in Job sinks deeply into the consciousness of subsequent writers, as the "foundation stories" of so many fantasy tales attest.

4. So much so that care must be taken in the planning of worship's music to avoid manipulation. Music's emotional push and pull is one reason why discussions about "worship" in the church grow so heated. Instruments, time signatures, rhythms, lyrics, and volume all come under scrutiny; conversation can quickly degenerate into condemnation, losing the why and what of worship beneath the how. The irony of such a progression has been

duly catalogued and begs for temperate treatment, particularly in the area of music.

Further, as important as music is for worship, it cannot be simply equated with worship. When the community gathers, it will sing, but its worship will be more textured and include a number of activities, pursuits, and postures.

5. Another way to discuss this is with the concepts of immanence and transcendence. Writing in a different context, Brennan Manning deals with their juxtaposition: "Transcendence means that God cannot be confined to the world, that he is never this rather than that, here rather than there. Immanence, on the other hand, means that God is *wholly* involved with us. . . . Disregard of God's immanence deprives us of any sense of intimate belonging, while inattention to his transcendence robs God of his godliness." *Ruthless Trust* (San Francisco: HarperSanFrancisco, 2000), 82.

Chapter 12: Table Grace

1. This explorer of the South Pole is quoted by Lennard Bickel in *Mawson's Will* (South Royalton, Vt.: Steerforth Press, 2000), 23.

2. In this passage, Matthew recalls the great prophecy of Isaiah. He is not alone with this interest: the prologue to John's Gospel has more on this image of light.

3. Robbie Castleman says worship is too often "designed to make people at home and comfortable, not holy and confronted." He advocates a recovery of holy ground: "To be awe-struck again and again by the Truth and Grace of God is good for our souls." *Themelios* 26 (3): 64. This moves the emphasis in worship from concentrating on music, skill, leadership, liturgy, technology, congregational size, quality of equipment, or a tight band to developing a profound sense of God's presence and activity. *That* happens when strong, proud, blind people finally come to their senses and see that God is spreading a table for those who had only earned the gallows.

4. Communities of faith form when disparate Christ-followers, fueled by the love of God flowing to and through them, gather in response to this call. Hospitality becomes a watchword (see 1 Peter 4:9 and Heb. 13:2) as a "love for strangers" (the English word *hospitality* translates from the Greek noun *philoxenia*, which means literally "love for strangers") emerges and spreads.

Markus Barth reminds us that "whoever sits at table with Jesus must also accept the other guests in Christ's company." *Rediscovering the Lord's Supper*, 73. It's an apt caution, since the Lord has a way of welcoming the foolish, weak, and lowly (1 Cor. 1:27–28), those Anne Lamott describes as "walking personality disorders," to join him. The sobering news, of course, is that those phrases describe *us*. Fashioning a Christ-centered, Christ-honoring community is labor intensive. But then, "apart from conscious and courageous decisions to seek out and to extend community, nothing important or lasting is likely to happen." Laurence Hull Stookey, *Eucharist: Christ's Feast with the Church* (Nashville: Abingdon Press, 1993), 152.

It helps to have a wide angle lens so that we can place ourselves accurately. This was Paul's intention as he addressed factious Corinthians. According to Gary Shogren, the apostle wrote to help them rise "above the local squabbles and jealousies of Corinth and [show] them how they fit into the redemptive history in which the whole church participates." This quote comes from an English version of his commentary on 1 Corinthians, *1 Corintios*, Comentario Biblico Iberoanericano (Buenos Aires: Ediciones Kairos, 2004). Lesslie Newbigin describes this community passionately as characterized by praise, thanksgiving, truth, concern for others, commitment to "the exercise of the priesthood in the world," mutual responsibility, and hope. *The Gospel in a Pluralistic Society* (Grand Rapids: Eerdmans, 1989), 227–33.

5. "Since we are Christians, then, let's beg the assistance of the Lord our God against the attractions of a life that it's stupid to love. Instead, let's fall in love with the beauty of the life that 'no eye has seen, and no ear has heard, nor has it reached the human heart. For God has prepared this for those who love Him' (1 Cor. 2:9). And God Himself is that life. I can hear you applauding. I can hear you sighing. We should be deeply in love with this life." From Augustine: *Political Writings*, ed. E. M. Atkins and R. J. Dodaro (Cambridge: University Press, 2001), 111.

Dan Schmidt has pastored churches in the United States and Latin America. He is the author of *Unexpected Wisdom: Major Insight from the Minor Prophets* and lives with his family in Pennsylvania.